*Training Retrievers
and Spaniels to*

HUNT
'EM UP!

Training Retrievers and Spaniels to

HUNT 'EM UP!

by
JOE ARNETTE
&
GEORGE HICKOX

SILVER
QUILL
PRESS

Camden / Maine

9   8   7   6   5   4   3   2   1

Silver Quill Press is an imprint of:

Down East Books

P.O. Box 679

Camden, ME 04843

BOOK ORDERS: 1-800-685-7962

Library of Congress Cataloging-in-Publication Data

Arnette, Joe, 1941—
    Training retrievers and spaniels to hunt 'em up! / by Joe Arnette & George Hickox.
        p. cm.
    Includes bibliographical references (p.).
    ISBN 0-89272-450-1
    1. Retrievers. 2. Spaniels. I. Hickox, George, 1947– II. Title.

SF429.R4 A75 2000
636.752'435—dc21

99-088304

Acknowledgments

A good many aged and well-worn sayings contain a core of truth. For those of us who write non-fiction books, very possibly the most important of these dusty, old chestnuts is a statement attributed to Wilson Mizner, who wrote, "When you steal from one author, it's plagiarism; if you steal from many, it's research."

Humans have trained hunting dogs for many centuries and left a record of their trials and errors for a substantial portion of that time. Thus, it reasonable to assume that there is very little new under the bright sun that shines on the world of working dogs. Add to that the experiences of two men who have devoted, for better or for worse, an embarrassing amount of their lives to gun dogs—reading, writing, talking, thinking, training, and watching them— and the line between plagiarism and research becomes impossibly blurred.

All people involved with gun dogs owe each other. Individually, these debts may be small; taken together, they are massive. No one intuitively understands gun dogs or serendipitously figures out how to train them for upland bird work. Dog training knowledge is learned, it is experiential, and much of that experience is gained from others, who in turn gained it from their predecessors. People who declare that they have learned nothing from others, past or present, are either: liars or lousy dog trainers. Likely, they are both.

Since George Hickox and I make the forthright, and necessary, claim of being neither liars nor incompetents, our major problem is choosing whom to acknowledge for providing us with what. Quite often, information and techniques picked up over decades become so mentally mixed and firmly locked into a personal mind-set that it is impossible to recall where they originated. Who are the dozens of people who gave one or the other of us a choice training tidbit, a sound piece of advice, another way of looking at gundog behavior, or a solid kick in the butt to implant the foolishness of a transgression during our formative years? How many technical, semi-technical, and popular articles and books have we mined for bits of information? How many writings and authors are there whose titles and names and specific contributions have been lost to memory. To each question, we must answer, "Too many."

However inadequate it may be, a blanket "thank you" is all George and I can offer to those insightful scientists, trainers, and hunters, from distant years ago to days just past, who contributed so much to the collective knowledge we have absorbed. If we have stolen from you as an individual, forgive us our plagiaristic trespasses. Indeed, for all of the unacknowledged many out there, remember, it's research.

On a personal note, we offer our special "thanks" to Down East Books editor, Chris Cornell. Tradition in the book writing business dictates that editorial efforts should be acknowledged—a worthy tradition because editors earn the accolades they receive. In Chris Cornell's case, however, our recognition of debt goes beyond mere acknowledgment. Chris' involvement with this book can't be tallied in hours, days, or months. Rather, it is measured by a commitment that spanned several years. This book is Chris Cornell's as much as it is ours.

Both of us gratefully acknowledge all the contributions made by members of the Arnette and Hickox households. The level of tolerance, assistance, and guidance in these families has often reached a magnitude best described as astounding. But, most of all, we are blessed with understanding loved ones who have encouraged us in oddball pursuits and risky endeavors that frequently beggared common sense and endangered financial security. Mostly, those pursuits and endeavors had to do with dogs.

And what of our dogs? It doesn't matter that they cannot understand our gratitude. What is important is that we offer it to them—all of them—the good, the bad, the ugly. Each of them taught us something as unique as their own natures.

A Coauthor's Note

In this book, George Hickox and I are not presenting universal truths. There are none to present. For the most part, flushing-dog training methods are matters of opinion and judgment and, as such, can't be sold as gospel—or at least they shouldn't be. What we are giving you here are nothing more—but certainly nothing less—than our honest opinions and personal judgments based on actual, hands-on, in-the-field experiences.

Upland hunting dogs can't be trained by committee. Basically, flushing-dog training is a personal endeavor that involves one man or one woman teaching one dog to find, flush, and fetch birds. For that reason, we believe that it is best for us to speak to you directly. George and I prefer to think of you as a dedicated individual, and not casually refer to you as some vague "reader" or generic "trainer" who might spot-check this book to pick up a few hints. Likewise, you won't read that "the authors" believe something; you'll see "I" believe or "we" believe or it happened to "us."

In that same spirit, we have taken a different approach in our presentation. Rather than representing each chapter as originating from both of us, we felt it was more appropriate to give you the benefit of our individual strengths without burdening you with our weaknesses.

Thus I, the team's writer and amateur trainer, wrote the introductory material and the first five chapters, and did the initial manuscript editing. Professional trainer George Hickox handled the presentation of the more advanced techniques beginning with Chapter 6. (We will remind you of this shift in narrator at the end of Chapter 5.)

A final point. Throughout this book, George and I refer

to your dog as "he" or "him," in other words, as a male. This usage is simply a matter of editorial consistency and is not a reflection of gender preference by either of us.

Joe Arnette
Kennebunkport, Maine

Introduction
You **Can** Do It

Popular opinion holds that it is difficult, if not impossible, for all but skilled professionals to train first-class flushing dogs. Co-author George Hickox and I contend that such a notion is rubbish fostered by incompetent owners or third-tier trainers drumming up business. Top pros are the first to admit that there is nothing magical about gun-dog training, nothing in the entire process that prevents anyone from developing his or her own flushing dog.

The fact is that training a retriever or spaniel for upland bird work, while not simple, is a job that can be done by any amateur, dedicated novice, or even first-time owner. All it takes is a decent dog, a commitment to the goal, and a set of workable guidelines. If you can manage the first two, George and I will give you the third.

In North America, flushing breeds are building in popularity as solid choices for today's bird hunters—with good reason. Well-bred retrievers and spaniels are versatile dogs with flair and exuberance, and they will do anything a reasonable person could expect of them. They are highly trainable dogs that normally hunt for their owners, not for themselves, and they will find, flush, and fetch any American game bird. They are fun-loving dogs that fit perfectly into a home environment and are unmatched in the dual role of companion/gun dog.

Although hard statistics aren't available, it is arguable that at least regionally flushers equal or exceed pointers in number among active gun dogs. By way of example, as this book was being written, the Labrador retriever was declared the most popular breed in the United States for the seventh consecutive year. While some of this preference reflects current canine chic, much of it originates from the hunting public.

With the amount of huntable land and the size of game-bird populations both declining, upland hunters are increasingly dependent upon their dogs for successful days afield. In that same vein, the work of a polished flushing dog lends a unique element of pleasure to the bird-hunting equation, and for growing numbers of sportsmen and sportswomen, this satisfaction transcends the importance of a full game bag. For many hunters these days, it is the vision of fine dog work, not meat on the table, that draws them to the field. This book is designed for that type of hunter and for those who would become that type.

Although there are a good many gun-dog training books on the market, few of them deal specifically with the development of spaniels and retrievers as fine upland shooting dogs, and none treat the subject in a thorough and systematic fashion. Nor are they geared exclusively to American styles of training and hunting.

The bulk of the top trainer/writers who specialize in flushing dogs are British and, as such, approach the development of finished dogs from different angles than Americans. Since this is not the place for a lengthy comparison of styles from both sides of the Atlantic, suffice it to say that there is nothing wrong with the way the British train their flushing dogs—if you are a Brit. On the other hand, being hardheaded Americans, both George Hickox and I believe there are better ways for us to go about the process. By way of one important and fundamental example, traditional British methods do not stress the use of live birds in early training. In fact, on the other side of the ocean, live birds often play a relatively minor training role until a dog is well along in the program.

Conversely, American hunters and trainers follow the commonsense adage it takes birds to make bird dogs. From the time pups can run, their pressure-free introduction to birds encourages them to have a hell of a good time, to associate feathers with fun, to flush and chase and retrieve birds. Americans free-hunt young dogs on wild game, shoot over them, and allow them to retrieve killed birds much sooner than our British counterparts. In the States, we want enthusiastic dogs that love birds and bird hunting, dogs with style, an aggressive flush, and no retrieving problems. Knowledgeable sportsmen and sportswomen consider those features critical in a gun dog—and they develop them with plenty of birds.

There is nothing wrong with the way the British train their flushing dogs—if you are a Brit.

American hunters have different needs than our brethren across the water. We hunt different game, on different terrain, in a different fashion. To develop a flushing dog that will serve our hunting needs most effectively, our training methods have, of necessity, diverged from their British origins. However, to give credit where it is due, many of our finest retriever and spaniel bloodlines were imported from Britain, and much of what pioneer American flushing-dog trainers learned, they learned from the British. Americans have simply taken those methods, then modified and fine-tuned them in a variety of ways to meet particular demands. By the time you finish this book, you will be shooting upland birds over the proof that those modifications work.

The sole purpose of this book is to provide hunters with

proven and up-to-date methods for training their own flushing dogs. With that in mind, the following chapters are structured around four assumptions:

1. In large part, successful training begins with a well-bred dog from solid hunting stock.

2. Given proper guidance, a reasonable commitment of time and a willingness to understand their dogs, hunters can train those dogs to their full potential.

3. Problem avoidance—not problem solving—is basic to finishing a top upland flushing dog.

4. The majority of hunting dogs in the twenty-first century will serve as both companions and working dogs.

This book begins with a brief look at the human-dog relationship and its significance to today's hunting dog owner. From there, I offer retriever and spaniel breed descriptions, puppy-selection guidelines, what to look for and avoid in a breeding kennel, the pros and cons of purchasing a started pup, and the basics of feeding a hard-working dog. I talk about the first days and weeks with a youngster and discuss its housing, housetraining, and emotional well-being. I then turn to your dog's learning process, fundamental yard training, and introductory field exercises.

These guidelines and procedures are based on the concept that every moment with a properly chosen puppy establishes its lifelong, happy-but-subordinate-to-its-owner position in the human pack and is a critical part of its training as a good citizen and competent gun dog.

At that point, George Hickox will take over and walk you through the intermediate levels of bird work, formal patterning, the use of wind, and retrieving. He'll then move on to producing a finished dog that is steady to flush and shot, tracks and stops on running birds, and performs both marked and blind retrieves. In the book's appendices, George provides detailed information on basic nutrition, an introduction to training with electronics, and a discussion of the conditioned retrieve. The latter two subjects are appended not because of any subtle disapproval of them—quite the contrary—but because their application might be neither necessary nor advisable for all readers at all skill levels.

A point to note is that this book can be used to train dogs of most ages. If you own a well-bred but somewhat older retriever or spaniel, don't hesitate to use this program. For practical purposes, let's define "older" as up to about five or six years. If your dog is much beyond that age, you must determine if the time and effort involved in intensive training are worthwhile to you and, above all, fair to the dog.

Should you decide to train an older spaniel or retriever, you must keep several things in mind: First, just because your dog is mature and well-mannered around the house, don't be tempted to rush or skip training sequences. In other words, don't fall into the trap of thinking he will learn more rapidly and be easier to train. He will not. Older dogs carry the baggage of their years; they have habits and behavioral routines that might be perfectly acceptable in a casual pet of whom little is expected, but are detrimental to the development of a working dog. Certainly an older dog can be trained to hunt, but rarely is the process as easy as with a puppy.

In fairness, I must tell you what is not in this book. You won't find specific techniques for developing a field-trial competitor, though much of the training is similar. Likewise, you will find nothing on training a non-slip retriever; however, a finished, line-steady flusher can function perfectly well on waterfowl or dove hunts. Don't look here for shortcuts to honest and thorough training at all levels. Quick fixes don't work, and we don't offer any in this book. Nor have we discussed solutions to serious problems such as hard mouth, gun shyness, or aggression. Remember, our philosophy is problem avoidance, not repair.

There are no filler chapters on breeding protocol, litter care, brood-bitch maintenance, kennel construction, and medical problems (other than those relevant to puppy selection). This book is focused on understanding and training first-class flushing retrievers and spaniels.

Dogs are individuals, not generic soup to be made by adding a list of ingredients in a fixed order and simmering for a prescribed time.

I want to emphasize that this is not a "cookbook" detailing precisely when to undertake a certain exercise. George Hickox and I can tell you how, but no one can tell you when with any degree of certainty. Throw away any training book that says, for example, that at a given age or during a designated week or month of training, your dog should be performing a particular task. Dogs are individuals, not generic soup to be made by adding a list of ingredients in a fixed order, simmering for a prescribed time, then ladling out a finished product that will be praised by all who sample it. All dogs of each breed, even those within the same bloodline and litter, show behavioral variations that are occasionally subtle but are more often dramatic. A recipe that works for one dog may be a disaster for another.

This book provides a program—not a schedule—for American upland bird hunters, whether novice trainers or advanced amateurs, who want to bring their flushing dogs from know-nothing, butterfly-chasing puppies to finished performers in the field. George Hickox and I offer decades of experience formalized into what we believe are the best available commonsense techniques, presented in a fashion that is easy to understand. Our intent is to help sportsmen and sportswomen take the uncertainty and error out of training flushing dogs. Not the fun, mind you! Whether you're training or hunting, fun is the point of it all for you and your dog.

Although the waters of gun-dog training are not overly deep, they have been muddied by years of divergent beliefs, outdated or irrelevant methods, and obscure presentations. Throughout this book George and I have reminded ourselves of a statement (supposedly made by Mark Twain) that goes something like this: "The work of many writers has thrown much darkness on this subject, and it is probable that if they continue, we shall soon know nothing at all about it."

Both individually and collectively, George Hickox and I have done our best to bring light, not additional darkness, to the subject of training spaniels and flushing retrievers. Only you can judge whether or not we have accomplished that goal.

Contents

Part One:
Planned Parenthood

1.

Making the Most of the Human-Dog Relationship

In his book, *Man Meets Dog,* animal behaviorist Konrad Lorenz wrote, "One day, during a hard winter, a deer crossed our snowed-up garden fence and was torn to pieces by my three dogs. As I stood horror-stricken by the mutilated corpse I became conscious of the unconditional faith which I had placed in the social inhibition of these bloodthirsty beasts. . . . I was myself astonished at the absolute fearlessness with which I daily entrusted the fragile limbs of my children to the wolflike jaws."

Although Nobel laureate Lorenz's reference to "bloodthirsty beasts" and "wolflike jaws" are a touch sensational, his point remains secure. Well might he be astonished at the trust he placed in his dogs. But no more than the rest of us less lofty folk.

How many times have we seen a child pounce on a resting dog, knock the wind from him, and be rewarded for the insult by a lick on the face? How many times have we disciplined an errant dog without a hint of retaliation? How many times have we watched a sleeping dog twitching in a predatory dreamworld and thought, "I wonder what he is chasing?" He could be chasing anything—anything, that is, but us, his people. And that is what is most astonishing.

To be sure, "unconditional faith," as Lorenz phrased it, is the core of the unique alliance of mankind and the dog. No other species of animal is as inextricably woven into the fabric of human life. From wild state to domestication, from shiftless mutts to fine-tuned spaniels and retrievers, the human–dog relationship is unlike any other on earth.

> **To bird hunters, the facts of how wolves became dogs may not seem that relevant. The reality is quite the opposite.**

Canis familiaris, the domestic dog, was the first animal to result from the taming of a wild species and has a history that some experts believe goes back to man's dark and distant eras. Archeological evidence demonstrates that the human–dog partnership, particularly in terms of cooperative hunting, was well established at least 14,000 years ago, the time traditionally assigned to Fido's domestication.

But during the 1990s, modern DNA analysis stirred a new ingredient into the stewpot of dog creation, and it makes a strong case that the domestic dog is much older than 14,000 years. Data suggest that the original transformation from wolf to dog may have taken place 100,000 years back. Research has also confirmed what experts have long believed: that the wolf, and the wolf alone, is the forebear of the dog; that retrievers and spaniels—along with Great Danes, coonhounds, and nasty toy poodles—are wolves in dogs' clothing. Undeniably, the ancestral wolf lives on in today's dogs.

It is not surprising that wolves were the forebears of dogs. Wolves, like humans, are creatures with a natural bent toward sociability; both of us show basic similarities in community, family groups, and social behavior. Whatever the details of domestication, it is not difficult to imagine wolves becoming enfolded into the structure of human social groups. Over time, these wild dogs would have changed, or been selectively changed, to meet man's needs and better fit into human communities.

A number of theories exist on the hows and whys of the wolf's initial interactions with people. The relationship might have had as casual a beginning as wolves scavenging around human camps and being fed, loose cooperation on large-game hunts or, perhaps, the simple fascination of one species of social animal with another. Unfortunately, what happened will forever remain speculation. In fact, we will never know whether humans or wolves made those initial contacts and began the grand association that gave us the dog.

Some authorities believe that a major factor in the full domestication of the dog was the suppression and alteration of its "perceptual world." According to this theory, aboriginal dogs underwent a complete psychological shift from a wild-world view of danger, stress, and aggression to a tame world of docility, tolerance of stress, minimized aggression, and perception of humans as benefactors and pack leaders. Such a proposal seems not only logical, but necessary if we are to make the mental long-jump from a wolf's stalking, killing, and eating a wild bird to a spaniel's willingly finding and flushing a ring-necked pheasant; sitting at the flush and watching the bird fly off, then fall; and, on a specific command, fetching it to our hand with barely a feather ruffled.

To bird hunters, the facts of how wolves became dogs may not seem that relevant. The reality is quite the opposite. For gun-dog owners, the critical social element forms the basis of our cooperative, trusting, and affectionate relationship. Indeed, the importance of the social characteristics that the domestic dog inherited from the wolf and the change of its world view from wild to tame are key factors in the foundation of the human–dog union and, especially, the full-flowering of modern gun dogs.

We get along with dogs and can train them to do our bidding because their underlying social natures have been manipulated to allow them to fit comfortably into the restrictions of human groups. Dogs, via wolves, are mentally equipped to understand boundaries, limitations, and social behaviors. They function best in a clearly defined *pack* where there are straightforward rules and an obvious leader. When the top gun in a wolf pack says "No!" to a subordinate, he means it. Trainers must assume the same role as the pack leader, and their commands must have the same impact. A dog's world is small, his view of it limited, and his pack, which means his family, is at the center of that world. These facts give us a jump on the training process. Well-bred, temperamentally sound dogs will play by the rules as long as they understand them and know that in our pack, there is no choice but obedience.

Owning, training, and hunting a fine gun dog is not democratic; think of it as a benevolent dictatorship. There can be no negotiation of terms in training and obedience. Reasonable orders are given by those who purchase dog food, and they are obeyed promptly by those who eat it.

Quality hunting dogs are born with fundamental skills and the social backgrounds to accept training that will aim those skills in the right direction. It is up to trainers to utilize and enhance the potential that has been bred into dogs' makeup over millennia.

Owning, training, and hunting a fine gun dog is not democratic; think of it as a benevolent dictatorship.

The upshot, depending on whose evidence we accept, is that somewhere between 14,000 and 100,000 years of domestication have given us the dog as we know it. Several thousand years have been involved in its selective breeding, while a couple of centuries have gone into the honing of those superb dogs that work for us daily in the field and each night lie peacefully at our sides. The entire process is astounding. From the first wolf that entered a human's hut to the spaniel or retriever we will hunt tomorrow, the evolution of the human–dog relationship is without parallel. It has happened just once in Earth's history. Its like will not occur again.

Mankind and the dog have walked a long trail together, and each step has deepened the relationship. The wolf has become the dog. The epitome of wildness has been tamed to become friend and hunting partner. Domestication, we tell ourselves, has extracted the wildness. But has it? Behaviorist Lorenz learned that a hint of the wild lurks in every dog. And perhaps that is not a bad thing, for as Guy de la Valdene wrote in his fine book, *For a Handful of Feathers*, "Dogs, like men, lose their range and enthusiasm for life from having the wildness in them questioned."

In our relationship with dogs, we should never attempt to strip them of that subtle suggestion of wild enthusiasm. We must channel it, use it to our best advantage to extend our dogs' figurative range, and in the process, further strengthen the already singular human–dog bond.

2.

Making the Right Choices

Quality hunting dogs are made up of three elements: genetics, nutrition, and training. It's that simple and, at the same time, that complex. If any part of this critical threesome is sub-par, a dog's performance will be proportionately mediocre, particularly at higher levels of expectation.

Contrary to the old saw, all working retrievers and spaniels are not created equal. Sportsmen and sportswomen who have spent time around these breeds know they come in an array of talent. The obvious superiority of a few boggles the mind, many are very good gun dogs, while the bulk are average or a cut above average. Still others cannot begin to do the job expected of them, for no living thing can rise above the genetic potential with which it is born. If a dog's potential is limited, so will be its abilities, thus its performance.

The same is true of nutrition, the second element in the flushing-dog formula. The best genetics in existence won't keep a hard-working dog solidly on its feet, doing its job, without a proper blend of high-quality nutrients. From puppy to adult, there is more to feeding a hunting dog than tossing him a couple of cups of bargain-basement chow once a day. Even an exceptionally talented, trained dog can only be as good as his diet allows him to be over a long bird season.

But it is training, the perpetual bugbear of bird hunters, that is typically the weakest side of the flushing-dog triangle. The finest spaniel or retriever ever whelped, fed the finest diet ever invented, will not live up to his potential without appropriate training that channels all that high-powered talent into hunting for the gun. An untrained dog hunts in his own style, on his own schedule, at his own speed. He hunts for himself, not in willing partnership with his owner. A dog may look beautiful steaming over the horizon, but if he is finding birds in one county while his owner is in another, he is as useless as a dowager's toy poodle.

Undeniably, the keys to developing a first-class spaniel or flushing retriever are to buy superior genes, fuel those genes with excellent food, and give that genetically talented, well-fed dog the finest training possible. Upland bird hunters who take that approach with their flushing dogs are en route to experiencing the best there is in the realm of shooting sports.

The flushing-dog marketplace, with its breeds, dietary products, and training equipment, is large and diverse. Fifteen breeds of spaniels and retrievers—ten of the former, five of the latter—are currently listed as hunting dogs, and within each of those breeds exists a wide variety of different bloodlines. Primary dog nutrition and health supplement products number in the hundreds, while the volume of training items—from absolutely necessary tools to utterly useless gizmos—runs to the thousands.

The sheer numbers of dogs, food, and gear are daunting. But because this book is above all else a practical training guide for upland bird hunters, a complete examination of everything relevant to spaniels and flushing retrievers is unnecessary. For our purposes, some basic facts concerning breeds and breeders, the selection and purchase of dogs, your early days with a puppy, and feeding and nutrition will suffice. (Equipment needs are described in Chapter 4.)

Sorting Out the Breeds

Of the fifteen breeds of spaniels and retrievers recognized as hunting dogs by the American Kennel Club, a hunter on the lookout would be hard-pressed to see six of them during a year afield, with four being a more likely total. Spaniels such as the Clumber, Sussex, field (the *field spaniel* is a breed), American cocker, and Irish water—along with retrievers like the flat-coated and curly-coated—are rarely seen as working hunters. On the whole, these breeds have gone the way of fodder for the pet market, become darlings of the show ring, or never achieved any degree of long-standing popularity in North America.

This is not to say that an occasional representative of these breeds doesn't turn up in the American fields and woodlands. To avoid hate mail from fanciers of these dogs, I will be the first to admit that individual Clumbers, American cockers, flatcoats, and the rest can do an adequate and even excellent job on upland birds when properly trained. On the other hand, there is no doubt that these breeds are low-percentage choices for the serious hunter. The majority of individual dogs within each breed give meaning to the admonition *buyer beware.*

The remaining spaniels include the English springer,

Welsh springer, English cocker, Boykin, and American water. In the retrieving breeds, we are left with the Labrador, golden, and Chesapeake. From the right bloodlines, individuals within any of these breeds can perform in the field.

The Spaniels

Among spaniels, the English springer reigns supreme over the dynamic world of the "flush 'n fetchers" in numbers, versatility, and—some would say—wide-ranging talent. Few experienced hunters would dispute the English springer's claim to the title of "King of the Pheasant Dogs," though this level of skill extends equally to all other North American upland game birds, from diminutive woodcock to heavyweight sage grouse. But there is another side to this wonderful breed and, as usual, it involves the show ring.

English springers have diverged into field and bench lines so different in appearance, skills, and temperament that for all practical purposes the two versions should be considered separate breeds. Serious hunters may not be well served by springers out of primarily show-ring breeding. Conversely, field-bred English springers from the right kennel—and there are a lot of fine ones—will give hunters all they could hope for in both the field and the home.

Welsh springer spaniels have a reputation as nothing but poky, red-and-white English springers. Although that disparaging designation is unfair, for the most part, "Welshies" are often slower, more deliberate hunters, and in some cases they appear less birdy than their higher-voltage English counterparts. But such a moderated style may suit sportsmen and sportswomen who find English springers too hot for their liking.

The English cocker spaniel, often called a "lot of dog in a small package," is a breed generally thought to bear the stigma of show-ring ruination. And that is a sad fact for a sizable percentage of these dogs, which have been swept up in the rush to feed the anaconda appetite of the American bench and pet markets. For some years, however, a few kennels in the United States have been rebuilding the reputation of this small, but hardworking breed by importing solid hunting stock from top English bloodlines. Available in a range of striking colors from solid black and liver to blue roan, English cockers bred in select kennels and used under field conditions appropriate to their size can be very fine dogs.

Boykin spaniels, American originals developed in South Carolina, can be nice, versatile little gun dogs, but their limited gene pool is awash with a high incidence of canine hip dysplasia. Because of this debilitating disease, the purchase of a Boykin spaniel these days must not be undertaken casually and should involve research into kennels, veterinary hip certification, and legally valid guarantees of puppy replacement.

The primary drawback to the American water spaniel, another truly American dog, is the breed's limited availability outside its stronghold of devotees in the northern Midwest, mainly Wisconsin and Minnesota. Don't be fooled by this breed's name. These nifty, rich-chocolate colored dogs have more to them than a special affinity for water work, and they are quite capable of performing in the uplands. The American water is the only spaniel that has an undocked tail.

One thing to always keep in mind when selecting a breed of spaniel is the game birds you will hunt. Given the generally smaller size of English cockers, Boykins, and some American water spaniels, don't expect them to hunt sprinting pheasants all day long in thick cover over expanses of prairie—at least not with the speed and stamina of certain strains of bigger, leggier springer spaniels. The cocker was developed initially as a small-cover woodcock dog, while Boykins and American waters began their histories as duck retrievers. But with commonsense use, these smaller breeds will do anything a hunter could expect of them.

The Retrievers

Like the English springer in the spaniel world, the Labrador sits firmly atop the pyramid of retrievers. Again like the springer, Labs are all-arounders capable of hunting any game under any conditions and doing it with a degree of aplomb. Although most aren't enthusiastic thick-cover bashers like top springers, well-bred Labradors will deliver the goods in the field, then snuggle up to the kids at home. A point to note is that some field-trial lines of modern Labradors have a tendency to be stubborn, high-strung, and superactive, but these are the exception rather than the rule.

Labrador retrievers come in three primary colors— black, yellow, and chocolate—but all are the same breed. Black is the predominant color and shows little variation in shading. Yellows run from washed-out, almost white hues to deep, marsh-grass gold, while chocolates range from pale brown to near-mahogany. In recent year, chocolate Labradors have jumped in popularity, a preference in large measure focused around the pet and show market-places. Without leaping headlong into the complexities of color genetics in Labradors, I must tell you that any time dogs are bred strictly to achieve a color (especially a highly recessive color with a limited gene pool), there is often little regard for far more significant traits. Thus it behooves a gun-dog buyer to look closely at what he or she might be purchasing.

As a breed, golden retrievers have the reputation of being mild-mannered lightweights best suited for romping with children and riding around in slick cars driven by long-in-the-tooth preppies named Chip or Babs. Don't believe it. Goldens out of straight field stock can do yeoman's duty on most upland game birds. But choose carefully. Some lines are of pure show or pet breeding, and these dogs have been out of the field so long they can't find their food bowls, let alone a pheasant. In general, goldens are easygoing dogs that take well to training, but, as in most breeds, there are lines that belie the golden's pussycat reputation. Moreover, in certain types of cover, their luxurious coats are a maintenance liability.

In terms of numbers, Chesapeake Bay retrievers rank a distant third behind Labs, then goldens. While a degree of the Chesapeake's low numerical position in the retriever pack reflects lack of favor on the big-time field trial circuit, even more results from their being labeled the strong-willed, "tough guys" of the gun-dog world. And there is a measure of truth here. On the whole, Chesapeakes are rugged dogs with great heart and an unquenchable enthusiasm for work, but they don't mesh well with people of all personalities. In fairness to the breed, which has a lot to offer the right owner, today's Chesapeakes are not the aggressive, hard-bitten, hard-headed dogs of legend, and they respond well to a fair and balanced training program. Of the primary flushing-dog breeds, the Chesapeake is likely to be the least tainted by the show and pet markets.

I can't tell you specifically what flushing-dog breed is

best for you as an individual. That is a personal choice that will be influenced by what and where you will hunt, what overall breed appearance pleases your eye, and what sort of canine personality blends with yours. Your lifestyle is a definite factor in breed selection: a larger, more active dog would be a poor choice if you rent a third-floor studio apartment, are gone twelve hours a day, or hunt just a few times a year. On the flip side, if you are a rural type who chases big-country pheasants four or five days a week, it's more than likely that one of the smaller spaniel breeds just won't cut it for you.

If you are considering your first spaniel or retriever, or are otherwise inexperienced, look closely at the most popular flushing breeds in your hunting area. Invariably, there are good reasons why some breeds are favored over others for certain conditions. Talk to local hunters; attend flushing-dog hunt tests and field trials; read breed descriptions in books and specialty gun-dog publications. (For a list of information sources, refer to the Selected Bibliography, page 235.) Always keep in mind, however, that many of these descriptions were written by proponents trying to convince you that their choice is the best breed known to mankind.

Look at it like this: Say you talk to ten local flushing-dog owners—both hunters and field trialers. Nine of them run Labrador retrievers and English springer spaniels, but one elderly man with severe gout favors a lesser known breed. The odds clearly dictate that you should think seriously about a Lab or springer.

Buying a Dog

Purchase price is the cheapest part of dog ownership. Over a dog's lifetime, your costs for food, vet services, housing, maintenance, and training equipment will *each* build to a higher level than the original price of the dog. Added together, these expenses will typically tally more than the initial price of a pup—and perhaps even a started youngster—within a year of bringing the dog home. Moreover, the difference in cost between a professionally bred dog of proven lineage and one from a backyard breeder's unknown female can be less than a night out with the family at a good restaurant.

Think seriously about pups from repeat breedings, which provide a track record of their offspring's temperament, trainability and field performance.

When it comes to retrievers and spaniels, the old saw, "You get what you pay for," is virtually always fact. Although luck of the draw may allot you an acceptable dog from a marginal bloodline, far more often the up-front bucks you save by buying cheap will come back to haunt you in hidden costs, lost enjoyment, and perhaps outright heartache. At the very least, you'll be saddled with a dog that can't give you what you want.

So, once you have decided on a breed, both logic and long-range dollar value dictate doing some serious homework. Then you should seek out reputable breeders with a history of producing top-quality lines, and buy the most genetically sound and potentially talented dog you can find.

If you do not start with a good spaniel or retriever, you are already on the downside of the training game. Throughout this book, the assumption is that you are beginning with a decently bred dog, that you have made the right choice, as is said, from the get-go. If you honestly can't afford the price of a fine puppy or started dog, neither can you afford to care for or train him properly. If you are simply too tightfisted to part with the money for a good dog, all I can say is, "Good luck!"

Once you have decided to cough up the necessary bucks, here are some rules of thumb: All puppies are cute, but harden your heart and resist the first litters you see unless you know in advance that among them is the pup that you want. You can always come back to them. In other words, don't buy on impulse. Similarly, avoid gift dogs. Loving families and kind friends often believe that the ultimate expression of their devotion to you is a warm puppy. Once again, keep that heart hard, and make your own choice. Never—read that again—*never* buy from a pet store. These dogs are rarely from hunting lines and often come from puppy mills that are filthy, fetid factories dealing in quantity not quality.

Beware, too, of buying from newspaper ads. Successful breeders do not have to advertise in the daily rags. Quite the reverse; many top breeders of spaniels and retrievers have waiting lists for their dogs. An exception to the newspaper rule may be local, amateur breeders known to you at least by reputation. Although these breeders run small operations, some of them consistently produce quality flushing dogs. As always, use a newspaper ad only as an initial contact to be followed up with research.

Selecting a Breeder

Unfortunately, in the United States there are no certification programs for dog breeders or the kennels they operate. However, by that statement, I am not suggesting that breeders as a group are a bunch of crooked shysters bent on bilking an unwary public. Most professional dog breeders are ethical businessmen and businesswomen who want the best for their dogs and their clients. Remember, these folks have invested their lives in the quality of their dogs and have staked their reputations and longevity as professional breeders on customer satisfaction.

But the hard fact remains that the lack of a policed, nationwide breeder-certification program means that any unknowing or unscrupulous person with a half-baked bitch and access to a stud can sell puppies. Be warned, as well, that breeder advertisements which appear in magazines are personal promotions, and their presence—even in respected national publications—is no guarantee of quality. For gun-dog buyers, this translates into your assuming personal responsibility for selecting reputable, established producers of field-bred spaniels or retrievers, individuals with verifiable credentials that are backed up by client recommendations and proof of performance. Ask for a breeder's client list, and call the people on it. Talking directly to these customers is one of the best methods of getting accurate information on the quality of a kennel and the dogs it produces. If a breeder is reluctant to name clients for you to contact, my advice is to look elsewhere for a dog.

When considering breeders, whether full-time professionals or dedicated amateurs, keep your perspective as broad as possible. Don't look at just one kennel or a single line of dogs for an immediate purchase, especially if you are a beginner with little or no knowledge of spaniels and retrievers. Talk to a range of breeders and ask pointed questions about the primary characteristics they favor. Within each breed, the personality traits of various bloodlines can differ dramatically. These differences aren't necessarily an issue of good or bad, but they should be viewed in light of what characteristics will best meet your needs. Think seriously about kennels that emphasize the sale of pups from repeat breedings. This means that the sire and dam have been bred to each other previously, thus there is an existing track record of their offspring's temperament, trainability, and field performance.

If possible, visit breeders *at their kennels,* and meet their dogs, *both puppies and breeding adults.* This comparative shopping can provide valuable, often telling, information. Look closely at the cleanliness of each facility. Quality breeders keep clean kennels and never allow their dogs, regardless of age, to wallow in their own waste. Don't buy from kennels that are filthy. Unsanitary conditions are often a sign of unhealthy dogs that are vulnerable to disease and prone to behavioral problems such as caprophagia (stool eating), housebreaking difficulties, and a host of other neglect-related syndromes.

It doesn't require wide experience to look at adult dogs or puppies and determine which are healthy and normal. Well-bred adult spaniels and retrievers are friendly dogs with sound temperaments. In or out of a kennel, grown dogs should appear clean, confident, nonaggressive, and approachable. Pups should have shinny coats; pudgy, but unbloated bellies; and clear, non-runny, alert eyes. They should be active and curious, willing to come to the kennel door to see what is happening. Beware of litters that hang back, try to hide, or otherwise appear overtly timid and fearful of humans; odds are they have been poorly socialized and may never adjust to life as part of a human family or as a gun dog.

In that vein, puppy socialization is an important subject to discuss with breeders. Ask them how many times daily—and for how long—their puppies receive deliberate human contact aimed at socialization. Are the pups allowed to play outside of the kennel? Does the facility have a person whose job is to frequently handle, wrestle, and just fool around with the pups? Are the youngsters taken on field romps and walks around bird pens?

There is another side to the coin in selecting a spaniel or retriever breeder. Although it is possible that there are several reputable kennels within reasonable driving distance of your home, this is unlikely. In fact, your research may point you toward a litter that is hundreds or even thousands of miles away. That means you will see nothing of the breeder's operation before buying a puppy. The dog will come to you sight unseen—probably by airplane—having been picked from a litter at the breeder's discretion. You will have selected the breeder strictly by his or her reputation, telephone discussions, and prior-client recommendations. And that's fine. Don't be afraid of having a pup shipped to you. It is a common and perfectly acceptable practice *as long as you have done your homework and chosen a breeder whose commitment to quality gun dogs is well known and unquestionable.*

Regardless of how or where you buy your pup, you should be given registration papers, a pedigree going back at least three generations, a veterinarian's health certificate and vaccination history, and a written guarantee of physical and temperamental soundness. This last item should include an assurance of replacement or refund should the puppy prove to have the sort of flaw for which breeders are traditionally held responsible.

For example, you should insist upon certification that your pup's sire and dam are free of hip and retinal dysplasia. Hip-quality certification is usually done by the Orthopedic Foundation for Animals, or simply OFA, though Penn-hip certification is gaining in popularity. Some upper-echelon kennels also provide soundness guarantees for their dogs' shoulders and knees. If you have chosen a top breeder, you won't have to demand these assurances—you'll get them as part of your purchase. However, such breeder guarantees can create false expectations of soundness; because of the complex, multigenetic nature of some inherited defects, they can do little more than increase your odds of purchasing a physically and mentally healthy dog.

Selecting a Spaniel or Retriever Puppy

Conventional wisdom among the uninitiated holds that if you know "The Formula" you can unerringly select the top individual out of a litter of seven- or eight-week-old spaniels or retrievers. The problem is that there are more formulas in the gun-dog world than fleas on an egg-sucking hound. These magic recipes usually include tempting pups with a flapping or thrown bird wing. Supposedly, only the dogs that aggressively charge in and grab the wing—or pick it up and retrieve it to hand—are worth owning. Some old wives' tales favor the runt of the litter, others opt for the first-born pup, a few go with the last dog weaned. There are arguments for taking the most dominant pup, while another case is made for the most cautious. Females are better hunters, say some. No, say others, males are more aggressive bird-finders. The list goes on, and it is my contention that the bulk of these selection formulas are hogwash.

If there is one constant in a litter of pups, it is change—often day by day, certainly by the week. The youngster that today charges out for the bird wing may show limited interest in it tomorrow. A little Labrador that rushes the kennel door to greet you and lick your fingers might hang back on your next visit. This week's undersized springer may be next week's average pup.

Puppy tests can't guarantee a top flushing dog—but at the least they can increase the odds of your picking an animal you can live with.

Two-month old dogs are still developing, and the limited amount of information you can gain won't be very useful for predicting how good a gun dog they will become. When you purchase a puppy, all you are getting are generations of selectively bred genes. In other words, you are buying genetic potential—what could be, not what will be. There can be no guarantee of performance. In essence, you are taking home a pedigree attached to a bundle of fur.

My uncle and early mentor in gun-dog affairs once told me that picking a pup from an eight-week old litter is a crap shoot. As we looked down at his recent litter of seven wriggling pups, he said, "Given a first-class breeding like this one, if you don't care about color patterns or sex, just close your eyes and reach in and grab one. You've got as much chance of getting what might turn out to be the best dog as you have of picking the poorest." That was my uncle's way of giving a know-it-all kid a lesson in canine genetics and the generally random nature of puppy selection.

My uncle finished his monologue by offering another approach: "If a blind grab doesn't suit you, sit down in grass, play with the pups, and take the one that seems to like you the most, the one that can't leave you alone. Let the pup choose you." There is a measure of truth in both techniques, although there are some things you can do to fine-tune selection and increase chances of picking the puppy best suited to you.

Various methods of puppy-personality evaluation and aptitude testing have been around in written form for at least a century, and they likely were known and in use much before that. Then, as now, their purpose was to determine roughly which pups in a litter were best suited to an individual owner or to a specific type of work. In recent years, behavior, temperament, and personality-trait tests have been refined and are used for making the early cut in selecting specific puppies as guide dogs for the seeing and hearing impaired, herding dogs, law enforcement dogs, and gun dogs. They are also relied on for matching pups with people.

For example, regardless of its potential talents, a puppy that early on shows excessively dominant or aggressively outgoing traits could be a poor choice for placement in a family with young children. Conversely, an extremely submissive and shy puppy that lacks self-confidence might do well in a structured, predictable environment, but it would be a risky proposition for an avid bird hunter who would constantly expose the dog to new and diverse situations.

Most of the puppy tests assess behavioral factors such as degrees of sociability or attraction to people; levels of independence, dominance, and aggressiveness; and ability to accept physical and social dominance by humans. They look at a pup's willingness to work with people (by way of retrieving tests), as well as at their sensitivity to touch, sights, and sounds, all of which have relevance to the world of gun dogs.

Space prevents me from presenting a complete look at the development, details, and interpretation of these tests. However, public libraries of any size, bookstores, and pet-supply houses usually have a selection of books that will at least outline puppy aptitude testing. (See Selected Bibliography, page 235.) It would pay a prospective puppy owner, particularly a novice, to learn the rudiments of these evaluation techniques. They won't provide all of the answers—and they can't guarantee a top flushing dog—but at the least they can increase your odds of picking an animal you can live with.

3.

Dealing with the Newcomer

There are two stages of life with the lovable puppy you have just carried into your home: fantasy and reality. The first lasts about a half-hour; the latter endures for the rest of the dog's life. Fantasy is marvelous—the wonder of newish life snuggling up to you for warmth and security, the puppy breath and young smells, the tentative licks and nibbles, the eyes that speak silently of unlimited promise. Then the puppy wets in your lap. You put him down to dry yourself and he poops on the floor. Reality has struck, and you must be prepared to deal with it in a structured way that helps the pup learn about life with a minimum of stress or emotional trauma.

One of the most overlooked parts of puppy parenthood is advance preparation for the responsibility of dog ownership. Spaniel and retriever pups are generally easy to deal with, but an eight week old can't be left to its own devices for sorting out a new life. It can't be cuddled for thirty minutes, then abandoned and given the run of the house for hours while the family goes out to dinner. A new owner must think out *before* the pup arrives the details of incorporating the newcomer into his home and daily household routines. Even first-class spaniel or retriever puppies can end up as disasters if their housing, housetraining, and overall care are left to chance.

Questions must be asked, then answered, well ahead of time. Where will the pup spend most of his time? Will he live in the house or in an outside kennel? If he is a house dog, where will he take care of his bodily functions? Will someone be around to play with him, feed him, and let him out numerous times each day? Will he . . . Well, you get the idea.

If you intend to keep the pup outside most of the time, your kennel should be sanitary, escape-proof, and safe from the ravages of an increasingly full-of-hell youngster that will test everything. And, obviously, any outdoor facility should be adequately heated and/or cooled. Housing a pup in a kennel is fine as long as he isn't isolated from daily activities or left alone for extended periods. I can't emphasize this too much—dogs are social animals and require a considerable amount of company for normal personality development and long-term emotional well-being. Should you opt for kenneling your pup, make it a point to spend as much time as possible with him. Bring him into the house when you can, play with him regularly, take him for rides and walks, and let him meet people who will make a fuss over him. Treat him like the puppy he is—let him be young and enthusiastic, encourage his natural bent to be happy and friendly during critical periods of his maturation.

For the most part, the same rules apply to a dog kept inside the house. The main difference is that you have to decide—in advance—where the puppy will sleep and where he will be allowed to go within the house. The single best, trauma-free means of controlling a young dog's activities and, at the same time, beginning his training, is a travel or confinement crate. This basic piece of equipment comes in a range of styles from molded-plastic, airline-approved models to collapsible, wire-mesh kennels. Airline-approved crates, like those made by Vari-Kennel, are perhaps the most versatile, durable, and widely used of all portable kennels. They will serve for travel and temporary confinement throughout the life of a dog.

If you choose to crate-train your puppy, buy the kennel in advance so as to have it available from the moment you bring your dog home. When purchasing a crate, factor-in the rapid growth of your puppy. Either buy one crate that will accommodate a full-grown dog of his breed, or have two crates—one suitable for a pup, the other matched to an adult dog. The problem with putting an eight-week old pup in a large crate—let's say one that will fit a seventy-pound Labrador—is that he might sleep in half of it and poop in the other half. Dogs, even youngsters, typically will not soil their own space—unless they have too much of it. Then, accidents can happen.

It is a good idea to confine a pup in a travel crate during the overnight hours, at times when you are not around to supervise him, and—now and again—during periods when you *are* available. Along with easing the struggle of housetraining and saving wear and tear on your home, the crate can help your pup learn the basic, but important command, "Kennel!" as he accommodates to confinement. Each time you put your pup into his crate, repeat "Kennel!" in a normal voice. Once he is in, tell him he is a wonderful guy. Start this process early, and you will ultimately have your pup kenneling on command and not bolting out when the door of the crate—or car—is opened the merest crack. (Chapters four and six describe the details of introducing, then refining the kennel and release commands that you will use for the life of your dog.)

Reality is that a hunting dog will be confined during a fair amount of his life—under many circumstances, for a variety of reasons—and it is far less stressful if he learns to accept it early-on. Some professional breeders, especially those who ship most of their dogs to distant clients, give their puppies a crash course in crate-training prior to shipment, in order to ease the strain of travel. But most breeders don't have time for this nicety, so don't count on your new pup's being accustomed to confinement.

If your dog will be with you indoors at least part of the time, it is necessary that you housetrain him. Perhaps I shouldn't emphasize necessary; there are casual sorts who don't seem to mind dog poop in their living space. That's a personal decision, but should you be nonchalant about piles and puddles don't hold your breath waiting for me to drop in for food, drink, and pleasant conversation.

Luckily, most of us are on the other end of the elimination spectrum and follow the rule our mothers taught us— that there are specific places for performing bodily functions and other places where those same functions are not allowed. That is what your pup must learn. And *learn* is the key word. An eight-week old puppy doesn't enter a house understanding that he can't unload on a Persian rug. Other than his confined sleeping quarters, space is all the same to him. You will have to show him where he can go, and you'll need to make certain that he gets there on time.

From a pup's first day in your home, you should establish a relatively fixed feeding and elimination schedule. A pup should be taken out to relieve himself as soon as he is released from confinement in the morning, at least several times during the day, immediately after each meal, and just before he is bedded down at night. Don't dally over coffee in the morning before you let the pup out to relieve himself. To avoid accidents, your first obligation of the day is to your dog. Likewise, your final obligation at night is to make sure your puppy has taken care of his affairs. Very young dogs—let's say up to about three months—will commonly defecate twice (back-to-back, so to speak) in a short period. Give a youngster enough time to clean himself out, particularly first thing in the morning, or you might force him into an error.

When your pup is out of his crate but still in the house, watch closely for signs that he needs to go. The point is to avoid accidents, not clean them up. Urgent circling or sniffing are clear signals that he is about to let loose. At first, don't call him to follow you outside, or he may make a deposit en route. Pick him up gently, without frightening him in any way, and carry him to wherever you want him to take care of business. Use the same place each time, stay with him until he finishes, then praise him. Don't put the pup down, then retreat into the house to get out of the weather or watch the news. If you do, I can almost guarantee that he won't relieve himself outside, which means he will do so soon after he is back in the house. Or, he will use as his toilet the doorstep where he saw you disappear, a location he may continue to favor for some time.

Housetraining a normal puppy is often considered a major issue. It isn't, nor should it be thought of in that fashion. Like everything else involving dogs, housetraining takes a commitment of time, an awareness of your pup and his needs, and a ration of consistency and common sense. Most spaniels and retrievers grasp the housetraining con-

cept quickly; others take longer. Some puppies are 90 percent reliable at three months, most are house-trained by six
months, while a few are prone to accidents at a year of age.
Frustrating as pups that stretch out the process can be,
don't give way to excessive anger. A physically and mentally healthy pup, particularly one under six months old, is
not pooping on the floor simply to aggravate you—any
more than children soil their diapers out of spite. The bulk
of humanity would agree that only a ghoul would spank an
infant for making a mess in his britches, yet such punishment is common for puppies that make a mess on the rug.

Lavish praise for "jobs" well done goes a lot further
than misdirected, premature, poorly timed corrections.
Whatever discipline is administered—and a scolding is
usually enough—it should not be done at too young an age
and must be carried out only when you catch a pup in the
act. If you missed the signals, that's your fault. Don't take it
out on the puppy, which may have already forgotten what
happened. By the way, never rub a dog's nose in a surprise
he has left for you. It accomplishes nothing positive and
may encourage stool eating.

What should a puppy know when he first sets foot in
your home? In a word, nothing. You must teach him everything. What should you expect of him for a period of time?
Only love, which he requires in return. What is he capable
of at that age? Adjustment and learning. Remember, however, that he can make progress only if you take the time
and have the patience to teach him the rudiments, then the
details, of living with you—under guidelines you establish.
A spaniel or retriever that is properly, sensibly, and lovingly
incorporated into a household is off to a solid start and will
benefit from that good beginning throughout its life.

Dogs may have short attention spans, but they are endowed with long memories. As I said in my introduction, ". . . every moment with a puppy establishes its lifelong, happy-but-subordinate-to-its-owner position in the human pack and is a critical part of its training as future good citizen and top gun dog." Take thoughtful and wise advantage of a pup's early months. Once that period is over, it can't be recaptured, and any serious damage done during that time is often difficult, if not impossible, to repair.

Buying a Started Spaniel or Retriever

The focus of this book is to move you as gently as possible through each stage of flushing-dog training, from educating a puppy to polishing a seasoned performer. However, there is always the option of buying a dog whose training has already begun. In fact, a started spaniel or retriever is an excellent choice for sportsmen who, for a number of reasons, may prefer to deal with a somewhat older animal.

Started dogs are exactly what their name implies; dogs roughly eight months to eighteen months old that have had some basic obedience training and have been introduced to the fundamentals of hunting. Typically, these dogs have been exposed to birds, gunfire, patterning, and retrieving. How much they know will vary with the individual animal, its age, its maturity level, how rapidly it progresses in training, and the preferences of the breeder. Remember, I am not talking about a *finished* dog, but one whose training has just begun. Even limited experience, however, can be a legitimate leg-up from several angles.

By choosing a slightly older dog, you greatly increase the odds of getting an animal with the skills and willingness to perform that you're looking for. In starting a puppy, the breeder has rolled the dice for you and formed a realistic assessment of the dog's field potential. He can demonstrate that the dog has no obvious physical or behavioral faults—or problems with birds, gunfire, or retrieving. Basically, what you see is what you get. And, if you have done your homework in selecting a breeder/trainer, what you get is usually a bargain, given the time and effort that has been put into a typical started dog.

Just because you buy a "started dog," you can't expect to bring him home in the morning and put him down to hunt in the afternoon.

There are a couple of things to keep in mind when considering a professionally started spaniel or retriever. One of those is cost. You will have to root around deeper in your wallet to find the price of an older dog. Trainers have to recover the food and health costs incurred by keeping dogs for the additional months required to evaluate their potential, then begin training them. Kennel operators have to factor in their personal time, the salaries of assistants, the maintenance of training grounds and equipment, and the cost of training birds. (As noted earlier, turning spaniels and retrievers into first-class flushing dogs requires a lot of birds, and the cost of buying or raising them builds rapidly.)

How much more will you have to pay? The amount varies considerably from dog to dog, kennel to kennel, and even region to region. However, if a professionally bred retriever pup from excellent field lines costs you $600, a one-year-old professionally started dog of similar breeding might run three to five times that.

Here is a bit of advice that you would do well to heed
when considering a started dog: To avoid hassles—and the
world of started dogs is rife with them—visit the kennel to
get a general sense of conditions there (just as I recom-
mended in the section on puppies). Look specifically and
closely at the dog being offered for sale. Any reputable
trainer should willingly demonstrate what the dog is pur-
ported to know and what you would be paying for.
Should a trainer show any reluctance to put the dog
through its paces, *walk away* because you are about to get
burned. The one exception to the necessity of seeing a
started dog in action before purchasing one is when you're
dealing with a kennel and breeder you know well or with
an operation whose reputation for fine dogs and honesty
is beyond reproach.

If you are thinking about a started dog, understand that
you probably won't be looking at the cream-of-the-crop.
(Breeders often keep top prospects for themselves or for
heavy-hitter, field-trial clients.) But, don't be suckered into
paying big bucks for a breeder's reject. Some professionals
view the hunting market as a convenient "dumping
ground" for dogs they judge to be noncompetitive on the
field-trial circuit. Now, some of these animals may make
fine personal gun dogs and can be a good choice for the
non-trialing hunter. The very traits that cause a particular
dog to fail as a competitive prospect—like a lack of sufficient size, speed, or aggressive style—may actually be desirable in hunting situations. At worst, they may simply be
irrelevant.

However, more than a few trial rejects have personality
problems that stem from trainers essentially short-circuiting
the critical puppy-development process by pushing youngsters too hard, too fast. In the rush for competitive success,

pups can be drilled under high levels of pressure that some of them can't handle. The result can be a hard case (an amateur's nightmare) or a dog that works only from fear of punishment. Even though such a started dog may perform adequately in the field, he will lack the typically good retriever/spaniel personality or even basic temperamental soundness. One way to better your odds with a started dog is to buy from a breeder/trainer who specializes in producing them for upland bird hunters. Under any circumstances, you should know up front exactly what you are purchasing.

Something else to keep firmly in mind is that just because a dog is started, you can't expect to bring him home in the morning and put him down to hunt in the afternoon. A few years ago, I ran into a fellow who did exactly that. Two hours away from the breeder's kennel, he buckled an electronic collar onto a nicely started, year-old dog and cut him loose on an endless vista of rolling hills. According to this lamebrain handler, the confused and badly spooked youngster rocketed off amid a flurry of electronically induced yelps. The man watched helplessly as $3,000 worth of dog and snazzy electronics disappeared over a distant hill, never to be seen again. My hope is that some deserving soul with more brains than bucks found the dog and gave it a good life.

A started dog has been introduced to the hunting game, *but it is not a hunter.* As much as anything, a newly purchased dog is a scared, off-balance youngster thrown into the company of total strangers. He needs time to adjust to new surroundings, people he has never seen, foreign kennel- or home-living patterns, and taking orders from you. You, in turn, need an equal amount of time to get to know him and make certain that you understand how to follow-up and maximize what the trainer has started.

Given a good beginning and even rough similarities between training techniques, you can use the information in
this book to advance and finish the dog regardless of where
he is in his training program.

Feeding a Hard-Working
Spaniel or Retriever

Unless a gun dog is in good physical condition, it can
not perform at its peak—whether training or hunting—for
any length of time. A working dog that doesn't get regular
exercise and is fed low-quality chow composed of little
more than ground-up chicken beaks, legs, and feet mixed
with cheap grains is going to run out of gas. Depending on
the individual dog, the breakdown may take an hour, a
morning, or maybe an entire day. But it will happen.

Look at it from this angle: Suppose that for a year, you
had no exercise and ate nothing but broccoli and bean
sprouts. Then at the end of that year, you entered a
marathon. How far do you think you would get?

Obviously, not very far. But too often that is precisely
what we hunters demand from our dogs. Worse, we expect
them to run the marathon day after day. And when they hit
the wall of exhaustion, we get angry and direct that hostil-
ity at the animals. Well-bred spaniels and retrievers are not
quitters; they have great enthusiasm, heart, and bird desire.
However, we must give them the physical means of maintaining their inherent drive. Part of that maintenance is an
adequate, ongoing conditioning program. At bottom,
though, "physical means" translates to "good food."

The North American pet-food market offers a range of
products varying from very poor to extremely high in qual-

ity. There are plenty of fully balanced dog chows geared toward athletic animals, and because gun dogs work hard, they have energy needs that only these upper-end foods can sustain. Grandma's lethargic lap dogs can do perfectly well on inexpensive, low-calorie chows because they have very different requirements than her grandson's retrievers or spaniels. Extensive veterinary research and field testing, however, have shown that such low-priced, non-premium foods are nutritionally inadequate for hard-going dogs.

Lethargic lap dogs can do perfectly well on inexpensive, low-calorie chows because they have very different requirements than working retrievers or spaniels.

On a national level, there are a number of name-brand foods that will provide your dog with what he needs to maintain health and maximum energy. Some regional companies also produce fine dog foods. The problem with choosing a regional product is that when you travel outside the manufacturer's distribution area, you have to carry enough food to last the entire trip. Remember, nothing will screw up a dog faster than a major dietary switch in the middle of a hunting or training trip, when he is already combating excitement, stress, and the digestive upset of new water sources.

Once you decide on a particular dog food, you can provide it in one of three ways: *free-feeding*, or putting out a large quantity of food and allowing the dog to eat when and how much he chooses; *food-limited feeding*, or putting out a fixed amount that the dog eats when he wants it; or *time-limited feeding*, which means giving the dog a fixed ration and about fifteen minutes to eat it before you take up the dish. The time-limited style is standard among hunters and trainers who need to control when and how much their dogs eat. The other two regimes—free-feeding and food-limited feeding—can create a finicky eater, a nibbler that picks at his food throughout the day, or a dog that eats on his schedule, not yours.

For example, let's say you have planned a hunt at 7 A.M., and unbeknownst to you, your free-feeding dog ate a double ration at 6:30. Chances are that after a half-hour of running, he'll slow down and get sick. If you are lucky, he'll blow the unplanned breakfast and gradually recover. If not, you might be in even bigger trouble. (George Hickox discusses these problems in Appendix A, "Nutrition Basics.") And how about youngsters? Ever try to housetrain a puppy that is allowed to eat however much he chooses whenever he chooses? He may get hungry at 3 A.M.; by 3:30, you'll have an ugly mess to clean up.

Here is a general set of rules for feeding a typically active spaniel or retriever: Provide your dog with an appropriate amount of chow on a fixed schedule. Pick a premium, calorically-dense kibble that is high in fat and protein, and if your dog does well on it, don't change. Dogs do not get bored with the same food year after year. If you must switch brands, do it gradually by mixing increasing portions of the new with the old over a week to ten days. Stick with dry rations. Canned or semi-moist foods are disproportionately more expensive, high in water content, and low in nutritional value. Minimize the use of table scraps; in larger quantities they can interfere with the dietary balance of your dog chow. Never give a dog sweets—especially chocolates, which may contain theobromine, a chemical that is toxic and potentially lethal to dogs. Don't work a dog for at least three hours after a meal, and wait at least one hour after a hard workout before feeding.

Don't give a dog of any age too much food. Obesity is the number one nutrition-related canine health problem in America today. Avoid it by balancing food intake, energy output, and the individual requirements of your dog. Feed with the goal of achieving and maintaining a weight that is optimum for your dog's breed, age, and activity level. By doing so, you can save yourself and your dog the misery of untold obesity-linked health problems. Contemporary research has shown that the food-bloated, corpulent puppies long considered to be desirable are anything but healthy. Fat, overfed puppies tend to become fat, chow-hounding adults that show a much higher frequency of debilitating bone and joint disease.

You can't control the quality and quantity of what your hunting dog drinks in the field, but you can make certain he has good water available at all other times.

Feeding a gun dog, whether an adult or a puppy, is largely a matter of a little experience and a lot of common sense wrapped around a few nutritional facts that begin and end with quality. Although in-store prices vary across the country, high-quality chows cost about twice as much per pound as cheaper foods. Anyone unwilling to give his dog the best available nutrition, however, doesn't deserve to own that dog. Any hunter who can afford a couple of shotguns, a truck, and all of the other gear we seem to need can swing a few extra dollars each month to feed his hunting partner a top ration. Besides, every cent that is put into food will be returned many times over in the dog's health and performance.

One more thing. Water, a fluid we take for granted, is critical to the development and continuance of all life forms. From lettuce to Labradors, water is the foundation of life as we know it, and without it life quickly sickens and dies. Don't think that I am making much ado about nothing, that I am overemphasizing such a commonplace substance. Fresh, clean, cool water is one of the most consistently overlooked necessities of a dog's existence. You can't control the quality and quantity of what your hunting dog drinks in the field, but you can make certain he has good water available at all other times.

Sound genetics and high-quality food are two critical sides of the triangle that yields a top upland flushing dog. Quality training is the third side. Let's get to it.

Part Two:
Kindergarten
Through
High School—
The Foundation

4.

Getting Started
the Right Way

I shot my first game birds over trained dogs as a youngster barely out of short pants. Since those long-past mornings, it has become absolutely clear to me that the best reason for hunting with a dog is to increase enjoyment of the sport. And training does that by maximizing a dog's genetic potential. In my view, hunting with an untrained dog is as much fun as walking uphill with sandpaper in your shorts. Conversely, I consider fine work by a well-honed retriever or spaniel as the essence of upland bird hunting.

A trained flushing dog is developed over time, with effort and dedication. How "trained" is interpreted, though, differs among hunters. A dog that an experienced sportsman considers barely started may be fully trained in the eyes of a beginner. Or, one hunter might care only about how many birds his dog produces, while another is concerned with how stylishly his dog finds those birds. What satisfies us as individuals depends on our knowledge, how deeply we are into hunting dogs, and what we ultimately

expect from them. It is equally true, however, that this satisfaction rises in proportion to quality of performance.

What George Hickox and I hope to do in the following
chapters is convince you that in the world of upland bird
hunting, there is no substitute for a well-trained flushing
dog. We want you to believe that if you follow our guidelines you will, in time, have a retriever or spaniel that not
only finds game birds, but does it with style. When you
turn the last page of this book, we hope you'll be a convert
who believes, as fervently as we do, that there is no reason
to be satisfied with a second-rate dog.

Flushing Dog Commands and Terminology

Virtually every profession, sport, and leisure activity
has its own specialized language made up of terms that, in
themselves, defy logic yet have very specific meanings. So
it is with flushing-dog training and handling terminology, a
jargon as obscure as that of any other undertaking.

You may quickly come to grips with "hard mouth" and
"pottering," but how about "blinking", "popping," and
"punching out"? Regardless of your IQ, you might never
figure out what they mean. Therefore, you must learn them.
By that, I don't mean that you should stop everything and
memorize the following definitions. However, you should
spend enough time on them to get a rough sense of their
meanings, then use this section as a reference as you
progress through the text. It won't be long before you will
be using terms like "marking a fall" and "taking a line" as
casually as you use everyday language.

Back—A retrieving command used to send a dog farther out and away from his handler in search of a dead bird.

Back casting—The dog's actions when he is seeking game (or simply running) *behind* the hunter rather than out in front or on either side.

Bailing out—When a dog is sent on a retrieve and stops his search without locating the bird. The dog has "bailed out" of, or "quit," the retrieve. This is not a common flushing-dog term, though you might hear it used.

Balking—When a dog has been given a command and refuses to obey (or obeys partially).

Blind retrieve—A training dummy, a planted bird, or a shot bird that the dog could not or did not see fall. Also, the act of retrieving same.

Blinking—When a dog knows game is present, but deliberately avoids or refuses to flush or retrieve it. A serious fault, blinking is usually, though not always, caused by the trainer.

Bolting—When a dog runs away to avoid control or correction.

Breaking—When a dog moves before a command is given. Usually associated with steadiness to a flush, shot, or retrieve.

Cast—This word has two meanings: Cast can refer to the distance a dog works from his handler while seeking game, e.g., "the dog's cast was too wide." Or, it can describe a dog's being sent to hunt or retrieve, e.g., "the handler cast his dog to the right."

Clipwing—A training bird, typically a pigeon, that has had its long, primary wing feathers pulled out or trimmed by scissors to prevent extended flight. A clipwing can walk and make short flights.

Cold blind retrieve—A controlled retrieve in which the dog has neither heard a shot fired nor seen a dummy or bird fall. Generally, the dummy or dead bird has been planted and the dog is handled to it.

Come 'round—A verbal command, or one given by two blasts on a whistle, that orders a dog running across the handler/hunter's field of view to reverse directions and stay within shooting distance.

Creeping—When a dog that is waiting to be sent for a retrieve, eases forward in anticipation. Often a prelude to breaking.

Dummy—A cylindrical training item of canvas, nylon, or plastic used for retrieving work. It is also commonly referred to as a "bumper."

Electronic collar—A remote training device that includes an electronic stimulus-receiving/delivery unit worn by the dog and a hand-held stimulus-transmitting unit operated by a handler. Also called an E-collar or a "shock collar."

Flyer—A training bird with its feathers intact. Capable of normal flight, the flyer is either thrown for a puppy to chase, shot for a dog to retrieve, or planted for a dog to flush.

Force training—In general, any training during which a dog is pressured, or forced, by the trainer to perform a task. Specifically, this training refers to the conditioned retrieve, a method of developing a completely reliable retriever. This latter process is also known as "force fetching."

Freezing—A fault, typically caused by the trainer, in which a dog refuses to release a retrieved bird. Some dogs that freeze on a bird neither kill nor damage it. They simply lock their jaws and hold on.

Handler—The person in control of a dog; the trainer or hunter who gives all commands and enforces obedience.

Hand signal—A directional hand and arm command that tells a dog to move right, left, or farther from the handler.

Hard mouth—A serious fault in which a dog chews,

mutilates, or otherwise renders game unfit for human consumption. As a rule, dogs should not break the skin of a bird while making a retrieve.

Heel—A basic command that tells a dog to walk in control (whether on- or off-lead) beside the handler, at the handler's pace.

Honor—To be steady to the flush, fall, and retrieve of birds worked by another dog.

Hup—The traditional, spaniel-trainer command meaning "Sit." This command is unique to spaniels but can readily be used for retrievers—just as "Sit" can be a spaniel command. The use of Hup or Sit is strictly a matter of personal preference, though some consider Hup to be the more forceful of the two words. The whistle command for Hup or Sit is a single, short blast. A visual command is the right arm thrust straight up. (See Sit.)

Kennel—A fundamental command that at first tells a dog to get into his kennel or crate, then expands to mean get into a truck or boat or whatever the trainer indicates. "Load" and "Get in" are variants of the command, though "Kennel" is most common.

Line steady—Refers to a dog trained to sit at his handler's side until he is given the command to retrieve. Line steadiness, or "steady to line," is a fundamental part of retrieving work and training a dog to be steady to flush and shot.

Lockwing—A live bird, usually a pigeon, that has its wings interlocked behind its back, rendering it immobile.

Making game—When a dog has either winded a bird or is working foot scent and is showing it through increased speed, excitement, and body language (such as a windmilling tail).

Mark—The precise spot, on land or water, where

thrown dummies or shot birds fall. Some field trialers use "mark" to refer to the dummy or bird that a dog sees fall.

Marking a fall—Refers to a dog seeing and pinpointing where a dummy or bird fell. Some dogs are better at this than others and are called "good markers."

Marked retrieve—A retrieve in which the dog has seen where the dummy or bird fell and visually/mentally marked its location.

Memory bird—The second bird, or dummy, to be picked up on a double, marked retrieve (i.e., while retrieving the first mark, the dog must remember where the memory bird fell). The term can also refer to a training bird dropped deliberately for retrieval later in the training session.

Objectives—Particular points, or distinctions from general cover types, where birds might be found or where experience has taught a dog to hunt. Hedgerows, ditch banks, marshy swales, and small clusters of apple trees are "objectives."

Passed bird—Whether in training or hunting, a bird that a dog has gone by and not flushed or retrieved.

Pattern—The way in which a dog covers ground to maximize its ability to scent game. The type of pattern a dog runs depends on wind direction.

Plants—Dummies or birds—clipwings, lockwings, or flyers—that are placed for the dog to find during specific training drills.

Popping—When a dog that has been sent to retrieve stops without a command, then looks back at his handler for help in getting to the bird. A dog that "pops" is typically the result of overhandling. "Popping" signals either that the dog has little confidence in its ability to find the bird or is accustomed to help from the handler.

Potter—To waste time reworking old scent, staying too

long in the area of a flushed bird, and/or fooling around with general smells in unproductive areas. Also, to work cover slowly—often walking or trotting rather than running—or walking constantly underfoot.

Punching out—The actions of a flushing dog that runs straight away from its handler without any attempt at working a pattern appropriate to the wind conditions. For practical purposes, a dog that "punches out" is poorly trained and out of control.

Quartering—A windshield-wiper hunting pattern in which the dog runs back and forth within shotgun range in front of the hunter. Quartering refers only to the pattern of a dog hunting into the wind.

Range—The distance at which a dog hunts, i.e., the distance between the dog and its handler. The yardage can vary depending on the cover being worked, but the dog must stay within reasonable shooting range.

Recall—The verbal and/or whistle command that a handler uses to call his dog to him. "Come!" and "Here!" are the two most commonly used recall words. Either will work, though "Here!" tends to be more emphatic.

Roll Whistle—This is a variation of the "Come round" command, but it is a continuous trill that, rather than turning a dog sharply, "rolls" or "bends" him into a more gradual turn back toward the handler. The trill is continued until the dog has turned the desired distance. This is a particularly effective command for pheasant hunters in more open country.

Runner—A healthy game bird that is reluctant to fly and is moving fast ahead of a trailing dog. The term can also describe a bird that has been wounded and can run but not fly.

Sit—See "Hup." With either "Hup" or "Sit," the command itself means that the dog is to stay put until released. "Sit" is the command most commonly used by retriever owners.

Steady to flush and shot—This phrase is usually shortened to just "steady." Either way, it means that when a retriever or spaniel flushes a bird, or hears a shot, he sits down and waits for the command to retrieve—or to move on if the bird was missed. Both flushes and shots are, themselves, commands that trigger the "Sit" response.

Sticking—This term differs from "freezing" only in degree. Sticking is when a dog is reluctant to give up a bird but does not refuse to do so. It also refers to a dog that hangs up, or "sticks," on a command such as "Hup" and won't move, even when ordered. Sticking is often the result of confusion and/or overtraining.

Switching—When a flushing dog is carrying a bird on a retrieve, finds another shot bird, and drops the first to pick up the second. This habit is undesirable; the first bird might be wing-tipped and run off, never to be found. Chronic "switchers" may also develop other retrieving problems. In retriever circles, switching means the dog "establishes a hunt" for one marked fall but abandons the search to hunt the area of a second fall.

Taking a line—This refers to the path a dog follows en route to a retrieve. A dog running a good line goes straight to his mark, whether bird or dummy, without wandering or deviating to avoid minor obstacles in his path.

Wild flush—When a bird, in training or hunting, flushes on its own, away from and apart from any action of the dog. A true wild flush is not the fault of the dog. Birds that flush wild are also called "volunteers" or "volunteer birds."

Wing guns—These are hunters or training assistants positioned at a given distance on each side of a dog's handler. The dog patterns at an appropriate range in front of the handler, roughly from wing gun to wing gun, thus providing them with a chance to shoot any bird flushed.

Required Basic Equipment

For the most part, gun-dog owners, whether novices or those with some experience, fall into two broad categories in terms of the quantity and functionality of their training equipment. In the first group are hunters who own no dog gear at all or, at best, a piece of baling twine for a lead. At the other end of the equipment spectrum are those who have attics full of entirely too much "stuff"—most of it useless. Equipment reality falls between these extremes. To be sure, you will need more than three feet of disintegrating twine, but you won't require a truck-full of extravagant gear. A six-figure income is not necessary to outfit yourself to train flushing dogs.

As I mentioned earlier, the gun-dog equipment marketplace is awash with gizmos, all guaranteed to whip your dog through training in the figurative blink of an eye. Keep in mind, however, that the bulk of these items are aimed at the well-meaning but unknowing sporting consumer, and they may have little to do with effective dog training.

For example, a retriever or spaniel doesn't care a whit if his retrieving dummies are exact, flesh-textured replicas of dead drake mallards. Such seemingly realistic touches will not make your dog a classy retriever. Only training can do that. An expensive, embossed-leather pigeon harness (designed to prevent flight) may look snazzy in your gear box, but locking the birds' wings costs nothing and is more effective. The same is true for hand-tooled or hand-braided collars and leads. They don't work any better than basic leather or nylon models and sometimes work less well. Buy the high-ticket items if you choose—we've all done it—but get them for yourself, just for the hell of it. Above all, don't try to wedge worthless or dysfunctional equipment into your training program.

The following list describes the essential gear that you *will* need.

Collars—Your pup can and should begin wearing a collar, at least for short stretches of time, within a week of his arrival at your home. Puppies grow rapidly, so you will need several sizes and types of collars. A cheap, lightweight collar is fine for getting a pup accustomed to having a strange object around his neck and for very early work, but when you start actual training you will need something more substantial. Depending on the breed and growth rate of your dog, you may require an intermediate collar before he hits the size he will wear as an adult. Heavy-duty, adjustable nylon collars with rugged snap-locks are a viable alternative for rapidly growing young dogs.

In terms of cost, usefulness, and durability, I believe that the best, all-around collar is a standard flat, one-inch-wide model with a D-ring sewn in. As for materials, it should be made from quality harness leather or two-ply nylon fabric. I prefer leather over nylon simply because leather is cheaper. On the flip side, plain or plastic-coated nylon collars come in reflective colors and are more easily seen on or off a dog. Whichever style you select, rivet onto the collar a small, metal plate that says, "Reward, Call Collect," then your phone number, including the area code. Do *not* put the dog's name anywhere on the collar unless you are interested in encouraging whoever finds your errant puppy to adopt him.

A choke collar is an optional piece of flushing dog gear. If you buy one, do so with the understanding that it has no use beyond backyard obedience training, particularly the heel command. A choke collar can be dangerous. If it's left on an unsupervised or off-lead dog, in or out of the house, the loose end can snag on protrusions and strangle a panicked animal. A choke collar should be placed on a dog when you need to teach it a specific, controlled task, then removed immediately when the session is over.

A variation of the choke collar is the "spike" or "prong" collar. This item incorporates blunted spikes that apply points of pressure when the dog jerks or strains against the collar. Some dogs respond well to a prong collar, though most don't require the added correction.

Leads—A lead is the same thing as a leash, though "lead" is the more accepted term in gun-dog circles. A standard training lead is six feet long and three-quarters of an inch wide, and it is made of sturdy leather or heavy-duty nylon, with a snap on one end. In addition to the basic version, I carry a short lead (sixteen to twenty-four inches long) made of leather, nylon, or braided cotton. These terminate in either a snap or a loop that can be dropped over a dog's head. Short leads are seldom used in training, but are handy for walking a dog to and from trucks, kennels and training fields. Because of their small size, they can be pocketed and kept out of the way while hunting or running training drills.

Check cord—This piece of equipment has its proponents and detractors, but when you need it, nothing else can function in its place. I consider it a fundamental training item. A standard check cord is twenty feet long, made from stiff, solid-core, half-inch, lariat-type rope that has a snap on one end tied on with a bowline knot. Don't worry, you don't have to hunt down a lariat, then try to recall how to tie a bowline. Check cords come ready to use.

Check cords are also available in varying lengths of flat, single-ply nylon webbing, half-inch marine line, and twisted polyethylene rope. For all-around practical use, I favor the twenty-foot lariat-type cord. Because of its solid core and stiffness, this rope doesn't tie itself into unmanageable knots, tangle on vegetation when a dog drags it during field drills, or wind itself around the dog or trainer. A nylon cord that is attached to a running dog at one end and is tangled around a human ankle at the other can burn that ankle to the bone in seconds. I've seen it happen.

Whistles—Training whistles come in a fascinating array, ranging from complex gadgets designed for use only by accomplished musicians, to mega-horns fit for calling elephants from great distances, to lower-toned, plastic "tweeters" made by Acme and favored by a good many spaniel handlers. Which are the best for use with flushing dogs in general? Without getting into that can of worms, I can tell you that regardless of their breed choice, most flushing-dog trainers opt for the lower end of the whistle-noise spectrum.

All dogs have excellent, albeit selective, hearing. An uncle of mine was deaf to the word "work" screamed in his ear, but could hear "whiskey" whispered in a thunderstorm at three hundred yards. Dogs, like my uncle, tend to hear what they choose, when they choose to hear it. It is a trainer's job to make them hear everything, at all times.

A loud whistle is no substitute for obedience training. Flushing dogs are hunted at close range and, therefore, don't require a police siren. A dog may respond to a super-loud whistle blast the first time or two, but if he formerly ignored a lower-pitched whistle, he will ultimately ignore one with more volume. Don't make excuses for your pup: Unless he has an inner-ear problem, he can hear a softly-blown whistle at a considerable distance.

For starting a puppy, the traditional plastic Acme spaniel-style whistle is a wise choice. It is inexpensive, has proven quite durable, and delivers a soft, peeping sound that won't aggravate your neighbors. Although popular whistles like the Acme Thunderers or one of the smaller Gonia series have more volume than you need, they will work. Just don't use them at their full capacity. Forget silent whistles. If you can't hear them, you won't know if they are working or if the dog is simply ignoring them.

Whatever type of whistle you choose, get one with raised top and bottom lips so it can be held by your teeth alone, freeing your hands for other work. And buy some kind of lanyard for hanging the whistle around your neck. Finally, always have a spare whistle—or even two—in your hunting coat and/or vehicle.

Training dummies—These are nothing more than old-fashioned, canvas boat bumpers remodeled to serve as retrieving aids. In fact, as I said in the commands and terminology section, "bumper" is a commonly used term for this item. A traditional canvas training dummy (or bumper) is white, measures about twelve inches long and two to three inches in diameter, and is filled with kapok for flotation. Smaller sizes are available for early retrieving work with puppies. Along with standard models, there are now knobby-plastic and foam-filled-nylon versions offered in a variety of colors. Plastic dummies are more durable and slightly cheaper than canvas models, though some brands are too hard and may discourage a dog from carrying them properly. Don't buy plastic dummies that have the feel of stone, but also avoid the ones that feel light as a feather—you won't be able to throw them any distance.

Although white dummies are all you need for basic training, other colors have their place. Remember, dogs see colors differently than humans. In cover, bright orange dummies, for example, remain highly visible to you, but are far less so to a dog, and that forces him to use his nose rather than his eyes. You should have at least four standard-sized dummies before you begin formal retrieving drills with a flushing dog. Most dog-supply houses carry them.

Dummy launcher—This is a simple, handheld device for throwing training dummies a much greater distance than any human arm can toss them. They are helpful for teaching longer marked retrieves on land and water, and for drilling-in the sound of a shot backed up with the excitement generated by a falling object.

Launchers are powered by .22 caliber charges that come in light, medium, and heavy loads that will propel a special sleeved dummy from 150 to 250 feet. Standard hand-thrown training dummies or bumpers can not be used with a launcher. For many years, the industry standard was set by the original brand-name model, Retrieve-R-Trainer. Although other versions are now available, some of them are made mainly of plastic. A safe bet is to stay with a launcher patterned after the solid, metal original. A basic kit includes a launcher, a cylindrical canvas or oval PVC dummy, some .22 caliber loads, and a cleaning set for under $100.

Training pistol—The device used to introduce a pup to gunfire, as well as in later training sessions, is almost invariably a .22 caliber revolver that fires crimped blanks. Some makes also come in .32 caliber, but they are rarely, if ever, used by trainers because of ammunition cost. There are at least a half-dozen brands of blank pistols on the market. Which one you buy should be dictated by how long you want it to last and how often you will use it; cheap models tend to fall apart quickly, usually in the middle of a training session. One of the best and most widely used blank pistols is made by New England Arms (previously sold under the H&R trademark). These revolvers are very durable, and with common sense care one of them will last throughout your dog-training life. Note that because blank pistols cannot fire real ammunition, they can be ordered legally through mail-order catalogs.

As an adjunct to .22 blanks and regular shotgun shells, 12-gauge blanks, called "popper" loads, can have a place in your training gearbox. When used as intended, they are a safe alternative to live ammunition. Their downside is cost—typically double that of basic upland bird loads—although handloaders can easily and inexpensively make their own, using a substance such as cornmeal as a buffer. Keep in mind that poppers are not powerful enough to operate semi-automatic shotgun actions; single-shot guns are safer on the training grounds anyway.

Bird bag—This item is exactly what its name indicates—a bag to hold training birds, primarily pigeons. You will appreciate the essential nature of this simple piece of equipment the first time you try to jockey three or four active pigeons, a shotgun, and a young dog on a check cord.

A functional bird bag should be made of lightweight, breathable material, and it should hang at your side by an adjustable shoulder strap. There should be a ten-inch, escape-proof, snap-top opening for easy access and an expanded, bellows bottom designed to keep four to six pigeons in good condition. The bag should have side pockets for gloves, fired shells, and dead birds. To prevent its loss in the field, thus saving yourself time and money, get a bird bag that's colored bright orange.

Grooming tools—By "tools" I mean a wire brush, a stiff comb with one end narrow-toothed and the other wide-toothed, and a quality mat-splitter. What does grooming have to do with gun-dog training? Nothing in and of itself, but regular brushing and combing removes fleas, ticks, and aggravating plant debris. It also promotes good skin and fur quality, and creates a generally healthier, happier dog. Begun at an early age, grooming, accustoms a dog to being handled and examined. Most quickly learn to enjoy it.

In terms of field practicality, little will shut down a dog—or at least cause him to lose focus—faster than a collection of sharp burrs in his armpits, in the groin area, or beneath his tail. Stick a burdock in your underwear, and you'll see what I mean. Left in place, large wads of hair and burrs can rub a dog's skin so raw that he can't run. They can also cause a form of localized bacterial dermatitis that may have to be treated with antibiotics. A mat-splitter is the most effective way of removing such serious irritants.

Remote bird launchers—This optional, and expensive, piece of training equipment allows you to launch birds or bumpers into flight at a distance, via remote electronics. I have included it, because some readers may have access to them through friends or training clubs. These devices are handy for marking drills and advanced steadiness training, but they are not absolutely critical for finishing a flushing dog.

Electronic collar—This, too, is a valuable, but optional training tool whose basic use is described by George Hickox in Appendix B, "Introduction to Training With Electronics."

General Guidelines—
Thinking Like a Trainer

Training a flushing dog is not hard-core science. Yet, similar to good science, it necessitates that you look past the obvious, that you deal with what is, with the reality of the dog that you see in front of you, not with what your human emotions say ought to be. In other words, dog training requires objectivity.

Dogs are self-focused. Regardless of how we view them, they rarely think beyond their own immediate needs, beyond what they want to do at any given moment. Dogs obey commands not because they know it makes humans happy, but because compliance works for them in a variety of ways from avoiding discipline to gaining rewards, including praise. A dog's fundamental reality is quite different than yours, and impersonal objectivity is not part of it. In the trainer–dog relationship, only you can provide that essential ingredient. Only you have the mental skills to remove yourself from what should be to training's real world of what is—and of why, when, and how much.

Gun-dog trainers, like any group of focused professionals, tend to toss out well-worn clichés to novices like weighty biblical injunctions. Although some of these pearls are time-tested and true, how much they contribute to the actual training process is questionable. With a few exceptions, I prefer to stay away from dusty old chestnuts.

One of the exceptions—a very critical one—says that during the first few months, puppies should be trained a little and a lot. This is another way of saying that you shouldn't demand too much and shouldn't overdo training; keep early sessions simple, short, fun, and free of pressure. It is far better to give your pup several upbeat, five-minute sessions each day than to load him up in one thirty-minute lesson. Always end each session on a positive note, with the pup clearly signaling that he wants more. But don't give it to him; tell him that he is a great little guy and quit. By adhering to the "a little and a lot" training philosophy, you are teaching your pup to enjoy every moment with you at the same time he is learning to accept control and absorbing basic commands.

Because dogs are individuals, it is impossible to forewarn you of every bit of trouble that you might confront with your pup. Where it is possible to anticipate problem situations, I will describe them, then tell you how best to avoid them. However, to solve those unforeseeable difficulties that always crop up, you will have to fall back on what you know about your dog, bolstered by common sense and sound judgment.

Here is another exception to my recommendation that you avoid trainer clichés. During the early stages of training, if you are not certain what is happening with your pup, return to simplicity; backtrack to a level that you *know* the dog understands. Don't be afraid to stop or retreat temporarily while you try to figure out *why* your dog is or is not doing something. In gun-dog training, taking a moment to think through what's going on is often the wisest choice. Indeed, as a trainer you must do more than ritually move through the steps of a program. You must learn to "read" your dog, first to understand what he is telling you with his body language or his direct actions, and second to know when to stop, back up, or move ahead. Don't make the mistake of thinking that behavioral signals go in just one direction.

As you learn to interpret your pup's actions, he is learning to read *you* and is forming lasting impressions of how what you do affects him. A good deal of his behavior may be a response to his interpretation of such things as your tone of voice and body language. For example, when you call him, does he run straight in with his tail up, then bounce happily around your legs? Or does he come in tail-down, moving slowly and fearfully? When you stand over him, does he grovel submissively, or does he wait with an attentive, confident look about him? Each bit of his behavior passes a message about how he views the immediate situation. A savvy trainer pays attention to these signals and adjusts his approach accordingly.

Be aware of the subtle distinction between correction and discipline: The first rights an error, the second punishes an infraction.

A few words here about praise and punishment. A widespread training belief, ingrained to the point of being gospel, says that there is no such thing as too much praise, that if a little praise is good, a lot is better. Before going any further, I want to emphasize that, with the exception of young puppies not involved in serious training, this belief is false. Human beings have an unquenchable urge to love-up their animals, which is fine in and of itself. The delivery of praise, however, must be controlled and done at the correct time, in the right place (the importance of timing and place in all facets of dog training can't be overemphasized), and in measured amounts appropriate to the individual dog. Keep in mind that dogs come in an array of personalities that respond to praise in quite different fashions.

Let's say that your dog has been performing a drill perfectly, so you tell him he is a great guy and make a big fuss over him. Then he ignores the next series of commands. This signals that your dog may not be able to handle abundant praise—or perhaps any at all—during training sessions. Such zealous praise may have created a distraction and caused him to lose focus. More likely, it passed a message that he was free to test your determination to demand obedience. With some dogs, you should save the "good boys" for the session's end.

Other dogs require varying degrees of praise to uplift them and keep their attitude positive during training. Certain dogs will fall apart without it. As a general rule, though, be conservative with praise; err on the subtle side, offering just a light stroking of your dog's head—at least until you know what is best for him. Once you have an idea of the kind of praise that works for your dog, you can use it to change his demeanor. Soothing, soft-voiced praise can calm an overly excited dog, while more active praise can animate a sensitive or lethargic animal. When you offer praise, do it for a specific act, at the place where that act occurred. In this way, the dog will understand that he is being rewarded for obeying or succeeding. Dogs usually tune-out generic praise that is scattered willy-nilly without purpose, or else they consider it an invitation to disobedience. In sum, the level of praise you use during training should make your dog easier to work with, not more difficult.

Punishment is the flip side of praise, yet there are many similarities in administering these opposites. Like praise, discipline should be used judiciously and timed perfectly, done in the right place and always be appropriate to a dog's personality and actions. There are dogs that seldom need anything more than a finger in their face and a gruff "No." Others require a good, scruff-of-the-neck shaking, while staring straight into their eyes and giving them a ration of verbal hell.

Under most circumstances, it is a mistake to administer harsh correction to a puppy. Dogs less than six months of age, and in some cases those that are older, may be permanently intimidated by rough treatment. People who beat up unknowing youngsters for puppyish transgressions fall into one of two categories and maybe both; they are expecting too much, too soon, or they require the services of a good psychiatrist.

An exception to the tolerance policy for puppy behavior involves biting. Because it can escalate in severity, even play-biting should not be allowed to continue for any period of time. If your puppy aggressively bites you or chews on you, tell him "No!" and snap his nose with a finger as you would flick a marble. If he persists, rap him under the chin with a knuckle, then pick him up by the scruff of the neck and tell him "No!" more sharply. Female dogs don't tolerate excessive biting from their pups, and you shouldn't, either. It is simpler to end biting early in your pup's career than deal with an adult dog that could hurt you.

At any level of training, punishment or reprimands should always be given at the spot of the offense. For instance, if you tell your dog to sit—assuming he knows the command—and he takes off deliberately, you must catch him and bring him back to where he disobeyed. Correct him there, so he can associate the correction with his act of disobedience at the place where it occurred. Reprimanding him elsewhere would confuse him, leading him to think that he was being corrected for what he was doing at the point where you caught him.

If you can't correct a dog at the place of his infraction and within a reasonable amount of time (perhaps because you couldn't catch him), don't make an issue out of it. By the time you corral him, he may have forgotten what he has done and may not have a clue why he is being punished. Better to let it go for that session and be prepared for disobedience the next time.

Regardless of what he has done or how badly he has aggravated you, never call a dog to you for discipline. Take my word for this. In his mind, your pup will think he's being punished for coming to you, not for the act of disobedience that occurred before. Punishment, like praise, must be something that your dog can relate to a mistake he just made. Remember, dogs are short on concentration but long on memory, which means that thoughtless acts can come back to haunt you.

When it is necessary to deliver punishment, you should know exactly why you are doing it, then make the correction quick and sharp. Don't lose your temper. Just get it done. Make your disciplinary point, then move on. Absolutely nothing is gained, and much can be lost, by punishment that is drawn out long past the point of effectiveness. (Note: From here on, you may notice occasional, deliberate repetition of points that are significant enough to deserve reemphasis.)

How Your Dog Learns

To avoid delving into the highly technical complexities of animal behavior, let's simply define learning in dogs as an ongoing series of *associations*. You establish these associations, and in the process train your dog, by conditioning him to respond to commands in a particular fashion. Then, you lock those responses into his brain by repetition backed with positive reinforcement, or reward. Negative reinforcement, or punishment, can eliminate undesirable responses. At its most basic level, conditioning (or training) is little more than your providing a stimulus, such as a command, and your dog's learning to provide the appropriate response.

Fundamentally, dogs makes associations in one of two ways: An extremely powerful experience, either positive or negative, can override the need for repetition and create an immediate and lasting impression on the canine brain. Let's say your dog investigated a box and found it packed with steaks perfectly suited to his palate. I'd bet the farm that the next time he saw a box, he would be into it looking for lunch. Conversely, if he stuck his head into the box and found a horde of hostile hornets, the odds are that from then on he would stay away from boxes. Although wild animals commonly learn the ins-and-outs of their environment in this trial-and-error manner, its relevance to dog training is limited to avoiding highly negative events.

The primary method of association used in gun-dog training is conditioning, which I have already defined as the linking of one event—the stimulus—to another—the appropriate response. Because those events will occur repeatedly at almost the same time, it is relatively easy for a dog to associate them. For example, if you push your pup's rear end down and immediately say, "Sit," you will find that over a period of time and with enough repetitions you will no longer have to push his butt down. The command "Sit" will have become the stimulus, and his obedience will have become the response.

Carried further, if you always bring your dog to a door to let him out and if you always tell him "Sit" at that point, he will eventually learn to do so without the command. In this case, the sight of the door itself is the stimulus that triggers the response. In sum, dogs are creatures of association and habit, and we establish those habits, or responses, by consistent, repetitive conditioning, whether in the house, yard, or field.

As you move into the more formal aspects of training, you will see that the concepts of association and conditioning are more than behavior-modification gimmicks. Consider a dog that is steady to flush and shot. He has progressively advanced through training, maturing from a pup to whom "Sit" was a meaningless sound, to a dog that is sitting on a voice command, then on a whistle. Ultimately, he will arrive at the point where a flushing bird or a gunshot, like the previously mentioned door, becomes an automatic command to sit.

Dogs, like most higher mammals, are very place oriented. They tend to identify acts or events, both good and bad, with the places where they occurred. Given the opportunity, dogs will sleep, eat, and take care of bodily functions in the same places. When they are nervous or frightened, they will seek refuge in the same places. Familiarity of place offers them a *safe zone* with its feeling of predictability, comfort, and security. A dog's strong sense of place plays a role in his learning by association and moving from basic to advanced training levels. In the sections ahead, both George Hickox and I will talk more about the importance of place-orientation and how you can use it to your advantage.

In Chapter 1, I said that every pack must have an unquestioned leader. In your pack, that leader has to be you. If you aren't in charge, your dog will take over that role, either subtly or directly, and you will be working for him. By the way, demonstrating that you are the boss doesn't mean that you should act like a prison guard. Done early, simple things like picking up a pup and turning him on his back, putting your fingers in his mouth, holding his jaws shut, and stroking his belly, muzzle and feet pass a clear message that you are bigger, more powerful, and in command. Only by being a strong, but fair leader can you take full advantage of your dog's social inclinations, his sense of place, and his willingness to learn by gradually constructing a series of associations that result in a bold, confident gun dog.

In general, training means that a dog will be taught, then made to do something he doesn't want to do.

In general, training means that a dog will be taught, then made, to do something he doesn't want to do. A puppy doesn't want to heel; he wants to run ahead. An adult dog really doesn't want to sit when he flushes a bird; he wants to chase it. Viewed in this way, training presents problems that dogs—as opportunists—will try to solve or avoid by taking what seems to them to be the easiest way out. But nature gave them just three ways of solving their problems: fighting, sulking, or running away. None of these options are acceptable to trainers.

What you must do is teach your dog a new means of solving the problems he will confront in training. In your pack, this solution is to obey your commands immediately, the first time you give them—not the second, third, or fourth time.

In the learning process, there are four basic stages that, over time, will bring a dog to the level at which he responds instantly to a command given once. For our purposes, I will refer to these stages as: *Show Pup, Stimulus-Command-Response, Command-Stimulus-Response,* and *Command-Response.* The first three stages lay the groundwork for the last. In this chapter, I will deal only with *Show Pup*. Co-author George Hickox will walk you through the details of the remaining three stages in Chapter 7, "Refining Basic Commands— Demanding Excellence."

Quite simply, these stages take your dog from the first demonstration of a command through intermediate building blocks of obedience to an immediate and appropriate response to a command. Whether or not a trainer locks in a command with these stages in mind, or does it unconsciously, the process should be the same. Whether or not a trainer uses traditional training methods or electronics, the process is the same. The order of the stages provides the underpinning for all basic training. They are described here so you can keep the sequence in mind.

Show Pup is exactly what it implies: showing, or teaching, your pup what a command means, what you expect him to do when he hears it. Your pup does not know English. Spoken words or commands are simply bits of noise to him. Therefore, you must show him that at the sound of a certain, unvarying bit of noise, he must perform a certain, unvarying act. For example, in and of itself, the word "Sit" means nothing to your dog, but when it is given repeatedly as you push his rear end down, he will begin to associate the word with the act. The more times you show your pup the response you expect when he hears "Sit" or any other command, the less work you will face later. All you are doing at this stage is making certain that the dog understands the command. *Show Pup* must be entirely positive and involve no discipline. Here, you are a teacher, not a disciplinarian. (Later in this chapter, I discuss the details of *Show Pup* relative to specific commands.)

Stimulus-Command-Response is the next step, where you first provide a stimulus, then give the command, and your dog delivers the response. Because of the many repetitions you used in *Show Pup*, your dog should already understand the meaning of the commands. The difference between this stage and *Show Pup* is that you now give the command just once. Let's say you are teaching your pup "Sit." You should apply the stimulus of pushing his butt to the ground, then give the "Sit" command once. If he doesn't obey—remember, because of *Show Pup*, he knows what you expect—correct him by forcing his rear end down again, *without a word*. Apply the stimulus again, if necessary, until he gives the response you want. By obeying your command, he has solved the problem, or turned off the stimulus, of your hand forcing his rear downward.

Command-Stimulus-Response reverses the previous order. You give the command first—again, just once. If your dog doesn't obey, correct him with the stimulus of more forcefully pushing his rear to the ground. The only way he can remove the stimulus is by obeying the command and sitting.

In both the *Stimulus-Command* and *Command-Stimulus* stages you can shorten your pup's learning time by applying continuous rather than momentary stimulation. This means don't slap your pup's rear end and tell him to "Sit." Instead, just push him into the sitting position by applying continuous pressure on his butt until he is down. This approach makes it easier for your pup to grasp the concept that the stimulus goes away when his rear is on the ground, that he can remove the stimulus by sitting. Ultimately, he will learn that by obeying he can avoid the stimulus altogether.

Command-Response is the final stage in the sequence, your goal that you will phase into smoothly if you have laid a solid foundation and not shortchanged the habit-forming repetitions of the first three stages. Now when you command your dog "Sit," he should immediately put his butt on the ground—without the pressure of your hand—and stay there until you tell him otherwise.

A word of caution bears repeating here: Youngsters can't focus on specific tasks for long periods. Keep your training sessions short. As I have said, both you and your pup will profit more from a few easy, brief sessions each day than from one long, tedious stretch of work. Be consistent, fair, and patient. Make sure your dog knows why he is being corrected, when you come to that stage. Be aware of the subtle distinction between correction and discipline: The first rights an error, the second punishes an infraction.

5.

The First
Six Months

This is the most critical time in your puppy's life; it sets
the stage for the rest of his development. During this
period, you must continue the socialization process that
was begun by the breeder. Because your pup's basic personality will be formed within his first half-year of his life,
you must use this time to create a confident and happy
dog. As I emphasized in Chapter 3, once the early months
are gone, you may have missed the boat. For the most part,
you will have to live with what you created, whether good
or bad.

Understanding the concept of socialization and its importance is simple and easy. Let's say that you brought an
infant home from the hospital, stuck him in a room, isolated him from life until he was six, then took him to
school. You can bet that his experiences in the first grade
would be daunting. It is no different with a dog. You can't
banish a puppy to a kennel or a distant part of the house
until he is "old enough to train" and expect him to develop

normally, let alone reach his full potential as a flushing dog and companion.

Your pup requires friendly, loving human contact—and a lot of it. He needs to see many different people, including men, women, and children. An easy way to give him this exposure is to make weekend trips to a shopping center. If you just stand outside a store, your pup will shortly meet a variety of adults and children who will pet him, make a fuss over him, and tell him that he is a great guy. But keep these trips relatively short. Don't overexcite or exhaust the dog.

If you have children, make it their special job to play with the puppy. Very little in life is more positive for a pup than being around happy kids. But don't allow them to be aggressive or bullying. Serious roughhousing with a pup is a bad idea for a number of reasons. Make sure that children keep play sessions, romps in the yard, and short walks gentle and friendly.

Socialization means familiarizing your puppy with different situations, as well as people. Take him for rides. Get him accustomed to traveling. Until he becomes too rambunctious, let him sit with you in the front of the vehicle; hold him in your lap and pet him rather than stuffing him into a crate in the rear of your truck, away from the comfort and security you provide. Perhaps you belong to a hunting club; if so, take your pup there on nonshooting, social days. The more new but not intimidating surroundings that your pup confronts, the more adaptable he will be as he matures.

At this early stage, exposing your pup to other dogs is a wise idea. Throughout his life, he will confront other hunting dogs, and he must learn how to deal with them appropriately. But this should be done carefully. If you have other dogs, don't kennel your pup permanently with one of them. Youngsters have a tendency to "shadow "or "tag-on" to an older dog if they spend too much time together, and you may end up with a follower who lacks initiative. Also, don't put your pup in contact—or, worse, kennel him—with a tough dog that will bully him or otherwise knock him around and leave such a negative impression that he will fear other dogs indefinitely. It may take a monumental effort to undo the damage caused by such intimidation—if, in fact, it can be undone.

In sum, while you continue your puppy's social education, make it easy for him to have fun and learn that life with you, indoors and out, is completely pleasant. You can't train your dog in a couple of months, so don't be in a rush to move forward into more rigorous lessons that involve greater degrees of pressure, correction, and discipline. Take your time during this early period. Without a solid foundation that creates trust, confidence, and boldness, your pup may never reach the level of performance that you envision for him.

Basic Training

There are four basic commands that you should use to establish control over your dog: "Kennel," "Sit" (or "Hup"), "Here," and "Heel." Because none of these involves birds or gunfire, locking them into your dog's mind is best thought of as yard training. At this stage, the order in which you teach commands is important. Think of it like this: It is easier to rein in and bring under control a dog that runs too big than it is to push out a dog that stays near you. Therefore, you should teach the command "Kennel" first because to comply, the dog must go away from you, however short the distance. In the same vein, you will teach the "Here" and "Heel" commands last because they involve coming to you and remaining close to you.

Unless he is told otherwise, your flushing dog's primary job will be to actively search for birds in front of you, not to stay by your side waiting for instructions. Teaching "Here" and "Heel" before introducing your dog to the rudiments of field work may confuse him and create problems with his range, style, and confidence. However, since you're not going to teach "Here" immediately, you must be careful not to work or run your pup in an area where he could be hurt if he doesn't come to you. Let him run free in fields and woods as much as possible to build his self-assurance, but always be aware of potential hazards. At certain times, for safety's sake, he will have to be on a lead or cord. Just getting him from your back door to your truck, or from the truck to a field, may require restraint to prevent him from splitting the scene.

Before you begin the "Show Pup" stage of teaching yard commands—and "Here" in particular—you should accustom your pup to the presence and feel of a lead and check cord. (He should already be wearing a collar.) A check cord is a fundamental piece of training gear, and your pup will have to become familiar with it. Moreover, because no commands or discipline are involved with his exposure to a check cord, it is best if he experiences it early on.

One way of effectively introducing the concept of a cord or lead is by putting the pup on a "chain gang." This training tool is exactly what its name describes: a group of dogs attached at intervals to a long piece of heavy-duty chain staked to the ground at both ends. (How long the chain is depends on how many dogs are involved.) At roughly five-foot intervals along the chain, there are sixteen- to eighteen-inch "drop chains" with swivel snaps that are clipped to the dogs' collars.

The idea behind putting a pup on a chain gang with other dogs is to let him gain confidence by solving his own problems, even as he is becoming accustomed to being

The chain gang builds confidence as it teaches dogs to accommodate to pulls and, thus, to being led.

pulled around. Imagine six dogs on a chain gang. When one pup fights, yanks, and lunges against the chain, the other pups tend to respond by lunging and pulling, too. After a time on the chain gang, however, each dog will start adjusting, giving with the pulls of the others. The chain gang confronts the pup with a problem that has nothing to do with his owner. He must confront that problem, deal with it, and learn from it. If your pup spends time on the gang, he will be accustomed to giving in to pulls—the concept of being led—which will make life easier when you begin teaching "Here" and, ultimately, "Heel."

As amateur trainers, most of you won't have a chain gang of your own, but you may have access to one. Pros in your home area or members of the local training or hunt club might let you add your pup to their chain gang. Or, you could join with dog-owning friends and make one for group use.

If you decide to put your dog on a chain gang, keep in mind the size and age of the other "gang members." Common sense dictates that you don't sandwich a fifteen-pound cocker spaniel pup between a couple of vigorous, eighty-pound Labradors. The youngster may be intimidated or, worse, hurt by the rambunctious pulling of the older, stronger dogs. A rough rule is to always group pups of comparable size. You can introduce a three-month-old youngster to the chain gang as long as he is matched with similar dogs.

Whether or not you use a chain gang, you can help your pup get accustomed to a check cord and lead in another way. Take a piece of clothesline about three feet long, and on one end tie a loop that fits the pup's neck loosely enough for him to slide his head out if he gets tangled as he drags it around. (Make sure to use a knot that won't slip or tighten if the pup gets hung up.) This lightweight loop lets the dog gradually adapt to having a cord around his neck without your saying a word or forcing the issue. Most pups adjust to the cord's presence within a day or two, then ignore it. You can introduce your pup to a light cord as early as three months of age. When he is a touch larger and sturdier and can easily tow a standard, lariat-style check cord, make the switch. (The timing will be dictated by your breed of dog.)

Let your puppy drag a cord—first the short clothesline,

then the lariat-style—during most of his early field romps. If you have more than one pup, or have friends with pups about the same age as yours, put cords on them all and turn them loose. Normally, the pups will start pulling or stepping on each other's cords. Just as with the chain gang, your pup will learn to give with the pulls, which will make your later work easier.

If your pup has never worn or been controlled by a check cord when you begin teaching "Here," he may make a negative association with its presence. If he has a cord slapped on him without a simple introduction or wears one only when he is being taught a command, he might decide that it is a nasty thing. But, if every time you take him for a run you put a cord on him, then allow him to race around and have fun, he will soon decide that a check cord is a good thing.

Once your puppy is completely comfortable with you and is well-adjusted to his new life (typically this occurs by about three months of age), you can begin focusing on the "Show Pup" stage of training the "Kennel" command. If he already sleeps or otherwise spends time in his crate or kennel, all the better; it has become a friendly and familiar place to him. If you have been using the word "Kennel" when you put him in it, that's fine. Nonetheless, don't stint on your efforts with this "Show Pup" exercise. Always remember that in this stage you are only showing your pup what the command means, teaching him to associate the word with a response. Keep the lessons positive, *with no discipline.*

Note that you should pick one command for each response you are teaching and stick with it. For example, don't alternate, between "Kennel" and "Get in" or between "Here" and "Come." If you choose to say "Sit," then "Sit" should be your permanent command. If it is to be "Hup," always say "Hup." Be consistent, and instruct your family members in the importance of this consistency.

To begin the "Show Pup" phase of the "Kennel" command, gently push or guide your pup into his kennel or crate while you repeat the command over and over. If he has already heard "Kennel" and has an inkling of what it means, he may walk right in. If he doesn't, don't yell at him; just repeat, "Kennel . . . kennel . . . kennel" in a non-threatening tone as you ease him in. Once he's there, tell your pup he is a good guy. Whether your pup has heard the command three times or three hundred, continue this exercise until he knows, without a doubt, what "Kennel" means. With multiple sessions and repetitions, your dog will soon come to understand the command and what is expected when he hears it.

With "Kennel," you are teaching your pup just one thing: to get into his crate or kennel. But putting him there doesn't mean that he will stay there. Because "Show Pup" involves no discipline, don't insist that he remain in the kennel, and never reprimand him for leaving it; he doesn't yet know any better. At this stage, you are simply teaching your pup to leave you and enter the kennel. Staying put will come later, when you begin to expect more from him. The "Show Pups" of kenneling are merely the first in a series of basic building blocks that, ultimately, will condition your dog to move away from you on command, go to his kennel, enter it, and stay there until you release him with a specific command.

You can introduce this release early on, after a week to ten days of "Show Pups." Pick one verbal command, like "Okay," stick with it, and use it every time your dog leaves his kennel or crate. Because your pup has no clue what the command signifies, you are not actually releasing him from the kennel at this point. Rather, you are taking advantage of your knowledge that he will turn around and run out as soon as he is free from the control of your hands. Anticipate his actions: the moment he makes a move toward the kennel door, tell him "Okay."

Use the "Kennel" command when you put your dog into a vehicle, a travel or sleeping crate, a kennel run, a boat or canoe—anywhere you want him to be. Never miss an opportunity to repeat the command, but don't get frustrated if he doesn't always comply. Again, in the "Show Pup" stage you are teaching, not enforcing.

"Kennel" (especially when it refers to personal and familiar space like his sleeping quarters), also introduces the idea of a *safe zone*, a place where nothing bad happens. In the "Show Pup" stage, your dog is learning, without pressure, that his kennel is such a place and that the key to it is obedience. Later, the safe-zone concept will be expanded to ensure his obedience to other commands.

This first learning stage should continue at least through the next three to four months of your dog's life, enabling you to get in thousands of repetitions of the "Kennel" command. Again, don't shortcut this process no matter how well your pup is progressing. By doing fewer repetitions of "Show Pup" before demanding absolute obedience, you run the risk of your dog's losing confidence or making the wrong associations with the command.

Once you understand how to teach "Kennel," showing your pup what you expect from "Sit" (or "Hup") is an easy procedure: Put one hand on his chest, and use the other hand to push down gently on your dog's rear end—use continuous pressure, not a momentary slap—while you give the command "Sit" again and again. Once your dog's rear is on the ground, reward him with praise or a small treat. This is not an exercise in seeing how long your pup will remain sitting. He is simply learning what "Sit" itself means. As with "Kennel," teaching him the word is the first building block in a process that, over time, will lead to his staying in that position. For now, be content that he sits at all.

Just as with "Kennel," you can introduce a release command after a week to ten days of repetition in the "Show Pup" stage of "Sit." Use the same command that you used previously, like "Okay," to tell your pup that it is all right to move. Now, however, you should combine the verbal release with a simultaneous physical gesture, such as a light tap on his shoulder. At this stage, don't force the dog to remain sitting if he tries to move. Understand that he will get up; anticipate when he will move; and as he does, give him the verbal and physical release commands. Above all, remember that you are introducing—not enforcing—the sit and release commands.

Teaching the command "Stay," so common in show and pet circles, is unnecessary. Later in the training process, when you begin to demand excellence on "Sit," you will expect your dog to remain sitting until you give him other instructions. Therefore, telling him to "Stay" is redundant.

To further develop the "Sit" command and the notion of a safe zone—and, at the same time—to take full advantage of a dog's sense of place, co-author and professional trainer George Hickox recommends incorporating a *training board* into your pup's lifestyle. This device is a piece of sturdy plywood, roughly two-feet square, with two-by-fours nailed along the sides to raise the platform off the ground. (Although the elevation of the board helps define its boundaries for the dog, some trainers use a more easily stowed piece of carpet or artificial turf for the same purpose.)

The training board provides a dog with a clearly defined place that he can easily understand.

No special techniques are required when using a training board, which is nothing more than a clearly defined set of limits that your dog can understand. Very simply, you do your "Show Pups" on the board, rather than the ground. In addition to using the device during regular training sessions in the yard, put your pup on the board before you let him out of the house or kennel to take care of his personal affairs, saying "Sit . . . sit . . . sit." When he comes in, put him back on the board and repeat "Sit." When you feed him, put him on the board and show him "Sit" just before you give him his food. Make sure that every time you push your pup's rear down on the board and command "Sit, sit, sit," that you follow it with praise before you release him. With enough repetitions, your pup will learn that the board is a good place to be. When he is sitting on it, he gets some form of reward. Along with its role as a place-oriented training aid for the "Sit" command, the board will be useful later, when you teach your dog steadiness to flush and shot.

You can begin the "Show Pup" stage of the command "Here" once your pup has learned "Kennel" and "Sit," has been on the chain gang, and/or is accustomed to dragging a check cord. As already mentioned, it is also best if he has had some field experience or, at least, is actively running and questing well in front of you. You don't want to create a pottering dog that thinks his job is to stay near you.

To teach "Here," put a check cord on your pup and let him run with it for a minute or so. Then hold the cord's loose end, and kneel down so you don't appear intimidating. Use the cord to pull the puppy to you. Don't yank or jerk him; just tug easily as you repeat "Here . . . here . . . here." Be upbeat, and sound positive. When he gets to you, praise him and/or give him a small treat. If your pup does not want to come to you, try backing up as you pull him toward you. No matter what he does, don't discipline him. Just keep showing him what the command means.

Above all, make sure your pup doesn't get the idea that "Here" is in any way unpleasant. As well as avoiding reprimands during exercises, don't confine your pup immediately upon ending a training session. He may characterize coming to you as negative, which will make your job far more difficult. Reward him with praise or a treat, and let him play for a moment before putting him up. Show him that coming to you is a *good* thing. And when you intend to put him in his kennel during non-training periods, don't always call him to you; at least half of the time, *you should go to him* and lead him to confinement. Whether you call your dog or go get him, give the pup about ten seconds of petting before you kennel him. If each time someone called you, he abruptly stuck you in a dank cell, it wouldn't be long before it would take an armed guard to get you there. Dogs may not be brilliant, but they are not stupid.

There is a school of thought that advocates teaching pups to stay close and respond to "Here" by hiding from them. Proponents say that this strategy will cause your pup to keep his eyes on you constantly and, thus, that he will not tend to run as big and will come to your recall command more readily. There is a small measure of truth in this theory. The downside is that hiding makes some young dogs very nervous, which can result in a lack of confidence in the field. It is much more effective to forget the shortcuts and teach your pup what "Here" means. Then, at a later stage, you can demand an immediate response.

As I mentioned earlier, you should not teach the fourth yard-training command, "Heel," until you've had your pup patterning, flushing, and retrieving birds that are shot over him. Although "Heel" is one of the four basic yard-training commands, you don't want to condition your youngster to walk by your side until he's comfortable out in front and on his own, looking for birds.

When it is time for the "Show Pup" stage of "Heel," use either a choke collar and a six-foot lead, or a self-tightening leather slip lead. Before you put either one around the dog's neck, make sure that it forms a "p" not a "q" as it hangs from your hands; this configuration will ensure that the collar or slip lead will quickly tighten and loosen as you make corrections.

You can teach your pup to heel on either your right or left side. The side that you choose is determined by whether you are right- or left-handed, which dictates how you carry a shotgun. Typically, right-handed shooters heel their dogs on the left, while southpaws position dogs on their right. Either way, be consistent.

Initially, work your dog in an area free of distractions. As you walk, your pup will almost certainly try to move out in front of you. When his head pulls ahead of your knee, give an upward and backward snap on the lead as you command, "Heel . . . heel . . . heel." Then, when his head is back at your knee, quickly slack the lead. Your snap should be clearly defined, but it should not be an attempt to jerk his head off. Nor should heeling lessons become a tug-of-war, with both of you pulling in opposite directions. Keep in mind that a couple of "Show Pup" sessions doesn't mean that your youngster will stop trying to pull away from you. Be patient: with enough repetitions of "Show Pup," the dog will soon respond and heel correctly.

Splish Splash

There is no particular time frame for your dog's introduction to water. Much of it depends on where you live and when you get your pup. If you are a northerner and pick up your youngster in November, seven or eight months may pass before you introduce him to water. In other parts of the country, he might be playing in rain puddles at three months of age.

As a rule, it is best to introduce a pup to water on a warm day, after he has been running and is heated up. The water you choose should be warm and shallow, preferably with a solid, gravel bottom and a gradual slope. Clear, slow-moving streams work well. Always avoid water with sharp drop-offs because when your pup takes a step and no longer feels the bottom, it will almost certainly frighten him. This can instantly create a negative association that may require months to overcome. Above all, never force your pup into the water. Sooner or later he will get there on his own.

If you have access to other pups or even somewhat

older dogs that already love water, all the better; bring them along. On a hot day, the seasoned dogs will jump in the water and swim, which will show your pup that there is nothing to fear.

Your youngster might not show any reluctance to enter the water. Some puppies take to it immediately, while others require extra help. If your pup simply will not go into the water or acts afraid of it, and there aren't other dogs to toll him in, you will have to get wet yourself. If you wade into shallow water, chances are good that he will follow you. If not, call him to you in an upbeat voice. If he still refuses,

Don't hesitate to get in the water with your pup during his introduction.

don't get angry. Call it quits and try another day. It may take time, but eventually he will get into the water with you.

If your pup has graduated from the retrieving corridor (see below—*Bringing Home the Bacon*) or, better yet, is readily picking up shot birds, try giving him a retrieve in the water. Sometimes the splashing of a clipwing will do the trick. But, don't throw your dummy or bird too far, and make sure that the pup's feet can touch bottom. *Gradually* increase the distance of the retrieves until your pup is swimming. Always keep in mind that water work, like all training, should be done in small increments.

Don't panic at your pup's first attempts to swim. The odds are good that he will awkwardly thrash his front legs, holding his head high above the surface, as if he were trying to climb out of the water. Although he may appear to be going down for the third time, he is *not* drowning. Remember, dogs must learn the rhythm of swimming, get accustomed to using their front and rear legs together, and understand that they are not in danger simply because their feet can no longer feel bottom. Some pups swim with confidence immediately, while others need more time.

After your dog has discovered that he can swim, gradually put him into situations where he can experience different types of water. He should learn to feel at home in rivers and creeks, large lakes, and small ponds.

Bringing Home the Bacon

Retrieving is something you will continue to work on throughout your dog's training program, and I strongly suggest that you turn to Chapter 8 (page 175) now, to get an idea of what's ahead. However, you can start your pup retrieving informally at an early age; three months is not too soon. As with other initial training drills, make sure that you give him enough time to get used to you and his new surroundings. For introductory work, nothing beats a retrieving corridor, which is a restricted area that gives you control over your pup's movements. Although you can begin inside your house—in a well-lighted hallway with one end blocked off—you will ultimately need to move outside.

You can set up a retrieving corridor in your yard in about thirty minutes, using a roll of sixty-inch-high, garden-variety, plastic-mesh fencing and a half-dozen six-foot

The retrieving corridor is the best means of introducing a pup to retrieving.

metal stakes. Whether or not your fencing is plastic, always use some form of mesh that allows your pup to see through. A solid material, like plywood, would make your corridor a dark and frightening alley. Stake the roll of fencing into a rectangle that is roughly twenty to thirty feet long, five-feet wide, and open at one end. Dimensions may vary, but if you can kneel at the open end and stretch your arms from one side to the other, you are on the right track because your pup won't be able to run by you. You should conduct all of your early retrieving lessons in the corridor, and your dog's introduction to birds should take place there, too.

Before starting your pup on retrieving, whether inside or outside, walk up and down the corridor with him. Let him check it out, smell it, and become comfortable in it. His first retrieving object should be a puppy dummy, a tennis ball, or a pair of tightly rolled-up socks. We'll call it a dummy here. Kneel inside the corridor's open end, and tease your pup with the dummy. Get him excited and make him want it, then toss it about two or three feet in front of him. Keep quiet while he runs to the dummy, picks it up and comes to you. If he doesn't want to deliver it, then you can encourage him or take a few steps backward as you entice him toward you.

Another bit of advice: Every time you throw a dummy for your pup, say his name. This will be his personal retrieve command. I advise against using "Fetch" because at times you may be out with other dogs that are trained to go for a bird at the "Fetch" command—a problem in the making. Conversely, the odds are slim that you will hunt with other dogs that bear the same name as yours. Let this early period work for you and help your dog connect his name with a retrieve.

Each time your pup brings the dummy to you or tries to get by you with it, gather him in gently without grabbing or threatening him, praise him immediately while he has the dummy in his mouth, then take it from him. Don't yank it away; just turn it or roll it out of his mouth. If he spits out the dummy before you can praise him, say nothing and repeat the exercise. Gradually, extend the distance you toss the dummy, but keep it short for a time—not much more than five to ten feet.

Because of the confining corridor, your puppy can't go around you or run away, thus you won't intimidate him with wild grabs or chases as you yell "No, no, get back here!" What you would mean is, "I don't want you to run away," but he wouldn't understand that. Your voice and demeanor might cause him to think that you meant, "I don't want you to pick up that dummy," a perception that could bring about a serious retrieving problem.

Most children love candy, but if they had to eat it all day, every day, they'd tire of it quickly. The same thing applies to puppies and retrieves, so *don't give your pup too many dummies.* In the beginning, three retrieves is plenty. As your dog progresses, four or five throws are enough. If you overdo the number of retrieves in a single session, there is a high probability that even an enthusiastic pup will get bored and quit. A bored dog is trouble, so, pay attention to your pup: if he shows any loss of interest—like dropping and leaving the dummy—stop the lesson. Don't give him retrieves for a few days, then begin again with just one or two. Always end sessions on a positive note so your puppy remembers how much fun it is to retrieve. Tease your dog with the dummy and make him desperately want one more pickup. But that one more should wait for the next time around.

Clients often ask trainer George Hickox how long these sessions should continue and when pups should be allowed to retrieve outside the corridor. There is no specific answer to these questions, but George's standard response says much: "If I were down to my last $10," he tells clients, "and somebody bet me that if I threw a dummy outside of the corridor my pup wouldn't pick it up and return it, I would take the bet and be assured of winning." In other words, George is never in a hurry to move out of the corridor, and you shouldn't be, either. Continue the sessions until you'd bet your last cent on your pup's willingness to retrieve. Repetitions in the corridor will condition your dog to bring a thrown dummy to you every time, and in the process they will prevent nagging pick-up or delivery problems.

When you do take your pup outside the corridor for his first unconfined retrieves, you should conduct these initial sessions on ground with low cover. Consider a golf course or a mowed lawn, though the area doesn't have to be that manicured. You want your pup to see precisely where the thrown dummy lands; you do *not* want him to struggle to find it in thick cover, get discouraged, and learn to quit on a retrieve. Start with short retrieves of ten yards, so that he can easily succeed in completing them.

When your pup begins retrieving outside the corridor, you should start his working drills in low cover.

Once your pup is retrieving clearly visible dummies at distances of twenty-five or thirty yards, you can begin making your throws land at the edge of higher cover—not in it, but close to it. If you pitch the dummy directly into the thick stuff, your inexperienced pup might fail to find it and give up before he learns to work out more complex retrieves. To avoid this problem, carry an extra dummy with you as a safeguard. If you inadvertently toss your first one into cover where your pup can't find it, drop the second dummy—without his noticing—close by, where he can quickly locate it. At this stage and for some months ahead, you want him to succeed on every retrieve and not develop a habit of making a token hunt, then quitting and moving on.

Some trainers advocate "line-steadying" a dog—making him sit and wait for the retrieve—from the very beginning. Such an approach is not part of the program described in this book. We recommend that you put off teaching line steadiness until you begin the process of steadying your dog to flush and shot, as George Hickox describes in Chapter 8. In the early stages of retrieving, you need not do more than tease your pup with the dummy, throw it, call his name, and let him go for it. All you are trying to accomplish at this point in your dog's training is building his enthusiasm for retrieving. Thus it is best to allow him immediate gratification and not force him to wait. It might turn him off or, at best, send a confusing message, especially when you add birds to the retrieving equation.

By line-steadying a young flushing dog before he is introduced to birds and allowed to chase them, you are almost certainly setting him up to fail. A pup trained in this manner early on knows that he is supposed to wait for the command to retrieve, but at some point he will likely lose control and break on these first birds, which will force you to discipline him. At this point, the risk—and it's a big one—is that he might associate the correction with the bird or the retrieve, instead of with his break from the sit position. Your goal with our program is to create a bold retriever that also has an unhesitant flush, not a dog that is uncertain of what you want from him or, worse, is confused or intimidated by birds. This is dangerous ground, and it is much safer if you do not line-steady your pup until later on.

The Pattern's the Thing

Springer spaniels tend to have a stronger instinct for quartering (working back and forth into the wind) than most of the other flushing/retrieving breeds. In all dogs, however, patterning and the appropriate use of wind is a combination of genetics, training, and field experience.

You can get an early jump on introducing your puppy to quartering by changing the way you take him for walks. Don't think of these walks as teaching drills. You are simply taking advantage of your pup's reluctance to move away from you, which translates into a desire to go where you go. You can begin short walks as soon as he shows an interest in following you.

Each time you have your puppy outside, wherever that is, never walk in a straight line. Wander from side-to-side, short distances at first—ten feet is fine—then gradually increase the length of your turns. Pat your leg, clap your hands lightly, or snap your fingers at the turns to encourage your pup to move with you.

Don't make a big deal of this, don't force your pup to do anything, and don't tire him out. Just walk with him. If he pauses, stop and allow him to investigate whatever grabs his interest. But when you move, do so in a zigzag pattern.

Along with instilling a habit in your pup, you are avoiding the notion that his life is straight ahead. These walks are nothing more than a casual means of maximizing the time before you introduce actual patterning.

Initial into-the-wind work, or teaching your pup the basics of quartering cover in response to a whistle, can begin early in his career. As soon as he becomes more adventurous and gains the confidence to move away from you freely, you should teach him that there is more to being out there than chasing butterflies. But read your young dog and don't push this exercise. Bolder pups often run out on their own, away from their handler, at three or four months of age. Others may require close to twice that time before they consistently leave the security of their owner's side.

As a start, take your pup to a field with low cover—a mowed pasture or even a football field will do nicely. There should be absolutely no distractions, and there should be a breeze blowing down the length of the field. Although there may be little for your pup to scent, working him into the wind allows him to smell what is present, thus reducing his tendency to cut behind you or roam far out to one side or the other. Initial patterning exercises are visual and auditory, and they do not directly involve your pup's nose.

With your dog off lead and out in front of you, raise your right arm straight up, and give two sharp, distinct peeps on your whistle. The moment you have your pup's attention, swing your fully extended arm down to the horizontal and walk rapidly to the right for about ten or fifteen yards. The pup should move toward you and follow you to the right. At the end of this first cast, raise your left arm, give two whistle peeps, then drop your arm to the horizontal as you turn sharply to the left at a slight angle ahead of your last walking line. Move ten yards to the left, give two peeps, and swing your right arm downward as you turn back to the right. In other words, you are moving forward, down the field in a zigzag fashion.

It is fine and often necessary with some dogs to exaggerate your arm and body motions, even to the point of *running* right to left and left to right. If your pup does not come toward you readily or shows signs of lagging, encourage him verbally, call his name, clap your hands, and give him a string of, "Pup. Pup. Pup." as you move. In short, do anything that triggers him to move back and forth across the field with you. But don't use your whistle to encourage him; save it for the two peeps that signal a turn. Remember, this is the first time your pup has heard a whistle. The sound won't bother him, but it doesn't yet mean anything to him, so don't confuse the issue by peeping at him to no purpose. In this exercise, you want him to associate the sound of the whistle—two peeps only—with turning and nothing else.

Don't expect too much from these patterning drills, at least initially. Some young dogs will act as if you are calling them to you, others will see this as an intriguing game and run around trying to join the fun. That's okay; just keep your pup moving. As long as he is more or less following your direction of motion, you are progressing. At this stage, if you can get four or five reasonable zigs and zags out of your pup during each attempt, consider it a success. Tell him he is a nice boy, play with him for a minute, and call it quits. Keep these patterning sessions upbeat, attention-grabbing, and short; continue for no more than five or ten minutes, or you risk losing whatever concentration he has given you. However, from now on until you begin formal pattern training, each time you are out with your pup, work him on into-the-wind drills.

After numerous days of repetition—how many will depend on the individual dog—your pup will begin using the whistle to anticipate your turn and move with you. If he has a strong quartering instinct, this casual exercise will develop that innate tendency in a pressure-free fashion. He will soon begin quartering in front of you without help while he is questing for anything that might intrigue him. For those dogs whose patterning will be more of a man-made product, this drill will begin to instill the habit of running at least a loose zigzag into the wind.

All you are doing in this exercise is laying the foundation for the formal patterning drills George Hickox offers in Chapter 6. But don't shirk on these initial quartering repetitions. At a minimum, your pup must be turning reliably to two peeps on your whistle before he can move on to advanced patterning.

Fun with Feathers

It is fundamental to all further training and to your pup's future as a gun dog that he does not develop a problem flushing birds. Most such difficulties are created when pups are confronted with live birds without first having had the proper initial exposure to this new and potentially intimidating experience. For example, you may be tempted to start your pup on a gaudy cock pheasant just for the thrill of watching him push it into the air. *Don't do it.* The raucous takeoff of a rooster may scare your young dog off birds forever. You must introduce your dog to birds with a logical, confidence-building, step-by-step approach. Although your pup might not be easily intimidated, it is better to err on the side of caution.

Once your youngster is delivering every thrown

dummy enthusiastically, you should introduce him to birds *in the retrieving corridor*. Along with the obvious benefits of control, your pup is already at home in this enclosure, has had fun in it, and is likely to have a positive association with anything that occurs here. Start your first sessions with a fresh-killed pigeon, chukar, or quail—birds that are small and easy for your pup to handle. Pigeons are usually the easiest to obtain, but whatever you use should be clean and unbloodied. Don't use a bird that has been frozen or dead a day or two.

Begin by throwing the first bird down the corridor, just as you did the retrieving dummy. Some pups will grab it without hesitation, while others will balk at the strange object. Don't be surprised if on this first toss your pup runs out, stops when he realizes that the bird is not his familiar dummy, then sniffs it cautiously and backs away. It might take a little time before a balky or insecure dog gains enough confidence to make the retrieve.

Try teasing a skittish youngster with the bird before you throw it. Don't overdo this and frighten him, just gradually build his excitement, get him bouncing around, make him want the bird. Above all, don't force the issue during his introduction to birds. Be patient with a less-than-bold puppy, and give him pressure-free sessions that build his self-assurance and allow time for his breeding to kick in, breeding that will ultimately drive him to pick up the bird.

Once your pup is comfortable retrieving dead birds, move to lock-wing pigeons that are alive but can't walk or flap their wings. Lockwings eliminate the risk that an active bird might spook your pup and make a negative impression on him. Use lockwings just as you did in the introduction to dead birds. When your pup is retrieving them consistently and confidently from the end of the corridor, you can move him to clipwings.

The correct sequence for locking the wings of a pigeon.

As noted in the glossary (page 45), these are pigeons whose long flight feathers have been pulled out, cut off, or bound with a strip of Velcro. All these methods prevent the birds from flying but allow them to walk and move their wings. (By using Velcro rather than actually removing the feathers, you can take off the restraint and reuse the birds as flyers.) Toss a clipwing to the end of the corridor. The bird will flap its wings and run, forcing your pup to chase it for the pickup. Once he is boldly retrieving clipwing pigeons in the corridor, you can introduce him to the flush.

The retrieving corridor is the perfect place to introduce your pup to birds.

Pen-raised quail are the birds preferred for this critical step in our training program. They are small and non-threatening, they tend to stay on the ground and run in front of a pup, and they have a relatively soft flush. If you can't maintain quail at your home, seek out professional trainers or hunt clubs that raise them or hold them in recall pens for their own use. Pointing-dog fanciers are typically your best bet as sources of quail.

With your pup near you, where he can see the birds clearly, release some quail from a pen or carrying container. As they walk away from the pup and begin to scatter, all those generations of selectively bred genes for which you laid out big bucks tell the dog one thing—to chase and get the birds. And if you did your homework and bought the right bloodlines, then introduced your pup to pigeons as I have described, chasing those quail is precisely what he will do. If, by chance, he catches one or two, before they flush, that's no problem, for he has been retrieving active clipwing pigeons.

Beginning trainers commonly see a conflict in allowing their pup to freely chase and flush birds. To many novices, the notion of gaining complete control over the dog may seem like training's bottom line, while encouraging a pup to engage in wild chases appears to fly in the face of achieving that goal. Establishing total control early sounds logical, but it isn't. Control means pressure and stress, and too much of either, too soon, creates many more problems than it solves. In the initial stages of gun-dog training, control is not the issue; building confidence and bird desire is the focal point. Stress can destroy confidence; birds can create it. By exposing your pup to feathers, by making him want birds above all else, his future learning and training, which include control, will go faster and more easily. Birds, in fact, are a safety valve, your hedge against mistakes.

At this point, whenever you put your pup into quail— and you should seize every opportunity to do so—you want him to go nuts and tear after them. You want him to chase and flush the birds as long as he can see or find them. Once your pup is fully confident and supercharged on quail, try him on other game. If you live in decent wild-bird country and your state laws allow it, don't hesitate to let your dog hunt the real thing. Wild bobwhites and ruffed grouse are fine birds that will get a pup up on his toes, and the diminutive woodcock is one of the best on which to work a young dog.

Wild pheasants can be a different story. As I said, a rooster's vigorous and violent flush may frighten a young dog if he hasn't been properly and gradually introduced to the experience. Always use caution and common sense when dealing with pheasants. If you introduce them, do so only after your dog has been flushing and chasing other birds for some time. And begin with pen-raised hens before you put out roosters. Let him get accustomed to seeing these larger birds and to hearing greater noise at the flush before he tackles truly wild pheasants. Should your pup show the slightest hesitancy around pen-raised birds, stop immediately. Forget pheasants for a time, and go back to quail.

Remember, until your pup has been introduced to gunfire, no matter how many chase-and-flush sessions you conduct, leave your shotgun at home and avoid any temptation to take a poke at tame quail or wild birds, even if the hunting season is open. There will be plenty of time to shoot over him in the months and years ahead. Indeed, that is the point of training your pup. For now, the purpose of these sessions is to develop a dog with confidence, boldness, and bird-drive, a dog that does not have problems with the flush. Allowing your pup to chase quail, then other birds, is a sure way to avoid any potentially serious difficulties with the whole process.

Before you move on to gunfire, your pup should be retrieving clipwings in the corridor—as well as enthusiastically chasing and flushing birds—with absolutely no hesitation. Then, and only then, are you ready to introduce him to the gun.

The Big Bang

There are many methods of introducing a dog to gunfire, but one of the best involves clip-wing pigeons. Clip-wings are favored for this exercise because their flight can be controlled by the number of wing feathers that are trimmed or pulled. These birds always come down, and you can gauge roughly where they are going to land, which is necessary because you aren't going to actually shoot

Your pup's introduction to gunfire should be conducted in an area of low cover without distractions. NOTE: For the purpose of illustration, the handler is shown launching the pigeon and preparing to fire the shot. Under most circumstances, an assistant should do the shooting at a distance.

them at this stage. Now that your pup is retrieving birds readily, you should be able to give him clipwings during gunfire sessions outside the corridor and be assured that he will deliver them.

For this session, you should again use a field with low cover and no distractions. Although you can conduct this exercise alone, it is best to play it safe and use an assistant. This person should be carrying a training pistol loaded with .22 blanks, and he or she should be positioned about a hundred yards from you and your dog. Begin by teasing your pup with a clip-wing pigeon; get him excited, but keep it just out of his reach. Launch the bird into the air as you call the dog's name (don't throw the pigeon in your assistant's direction). The bird will become airborne, but with its primaries pulled or trimmed, it will not fly high or far.

Because your pup has chased and retrieved many times, he should go after the bird aggressively. Just as the clipwing you've thrown hits the ground—*not when it is still*

When your pup and the launched pigeon converge, you or an assistant should fire a single shot.

in the air—your assistant should fire à single shot. By allowing the pigeon and your pup to converge at ground level at the moment the shot is fired, the dog will be completely focused on capturing the bird that's directly in front of him. Very likely, your pup will be so intent on the clipwing that he will not even hear the shot. Stage several of these sessions—let's say four to six, depending on how your pup responds—scheduling them at different times and/or on different days and   gradually moving your assistant closer to you as the lessons progress. The key word here is *gradually*. If you don't rush shooting over or near your pup, he won't remember when gunfire entered the picture.

Once your pup has experienced bird chases and is not perturbed by the sound of .22 blanks, give your assistant a shotgun with popper loads, and move him or her back out to a distance of a hundred yards from you and the dog. Now repeat the whole conditioning procedure gradually until the assistant is firing from a position near you.

Chances are excellent that you will experience no difficulties during your gunfire introduction, but if at any time, you should detect even the merest hint of noise nervousness in your pup, stop immediately. Give him a couple of days rest, followed by some dummy and bird retrieves in the corridor. Then begin the gunfire process from scratch. If, from the beginning, you treat your pup as though he might be gun shy, you will never have the actual problem.

Putting It Together

Because of your drills to this point, you know your pup has no problems with retrieving, birds, flushing, or gunfire. Now you should enhance his already positive association with—and thus his mental connection to—the entire package of experiences by allowing him to flush a dizzied pigeon, chase it, see it shot, then retrieve it. Again, you can conduct this exercise by yourself, but an assistant who does the shooting makes the process easier and allows you to focus on your dog.

To dizzy a pigeon, hold it in one hand with its wings trapped but its head loose, and place your forefinger over its crop. Letting its head hang down, whirl the bird around rapidly in small circles, then toss it to the ground five to ten feet in front of you, using a brisk forward motion of your arm.

The proper way to hold a pigeon for dizzying.

For this lesson, hold your pup by the collar about ten or fifteen yards away from your helper, and don't talk to the dog. Simply have your assistant dizzy a pigeon that is capable of full flight and throw it in the grass while your pup watches. Wait a few seconds until the bird is up and alert, then release the dog. When the pup makes the flush and is in full chase, your assistant should try his best to shoot the pigeon, but if he doesn't hit it, he should *not* fire a second time. If he misses, repeat the drill, one shot at a time, until he knocks down a bird for the pup to retrieve. Misses do nothing more than allow your dog a good chase. If he catches some of the dizzied birds, no harm done; he'll get the retrieves. By the way, once you or your assistant get the hang of dizzying pigeons, most of them will flush.

You should repeat this flushing drill, or your own variations of it, until your pup knows and loves the game and is ready to move on to the next stage of training. You can alter the distances at which you plant dizzied pigeons and can vary how far you let them fly before shooting them, which will determine the length of the dog's retrieves. From time to time, you or your assistant should miss birds deliberately and let your pup chase them. Periodically, throw a lockwing or clipwing instead of a flyer to keep your pup thinking that he can catch the bird. That, in turn, will keep his flush aggressive.

But don't overdo any of these sessions; keep them short, and limit the number of individual flushes and retrieves. In other words, don't bore your pup or turn him off with too many drills, overly long sessions, or excessively frequent lessons. Shooting just a couple of birds several days a week will suffice to keep his excitement level high and his associations positive. One pigeon is better than none and, in the same vein, a single bird is invariably better than ten in a row. Remember, this process is not an end in itself but an introduction that lays the foundation for further training.

You are now well on your way to producing a dog that will find 'em, flush 'em, and fetch 'em. At this level of training, you could take your pup on a limited wild-bird or preserve hunt. Although he is by no means under your full control (indeed, he will free-hunt most of the time), you could certainly shoot birds over him.

NOTE: *From this point on, co-author George Hickox will pick up the narrative and describe the more advanced elements of training a flushing dog.*

6.

Advanced Patterning and Using the Wind

For training purposes, patterning and using the wind are nearly synonymous. By using the wind, I mean the innate tendency of a dog to work wind currents and wind direction to best advantage in scenting game. Patterning is the physical means, usually taught, by which a dog puts himself in position to more effectively use his nose to locate birds. The type of pattern that a dog runs depends on wind conditions.

Your young flusher must learn three basic hunting patterns: upwind, crosswind, and downwind. In running an upwind pattern, also called quartering, the dog hunts into the wind, moving right to left and left to right in front of you within an established range. This hunting pattern is the most natural for a dog and is the easiest for a youngster to learn. That's the reason it is introduced early, as coauthor Joe Arnette described in Chapter 5. The formal upwind drills that I discuss here lay the groundwork for all the patterning that follows and, therefore, are taught first. Crosswind and downwind patterns require separate, different drills that should be undertaken after your pup has thoroughly mastered upwind patterning.

In gun-dog training, only when one element is successfully locked into a dog's brain is it time to move on to the next element. That is why you teach upwind patterning first and stay with it until the dog is working correctly and consistently. Then you can start crosswind drills. When your dog is proficient at hunting crosswinds, you can begin work on downwind patterning. In this chapter, my goal is to show you how to advance from one level to the next and, in the process, to develop a flushing dog that is competent at working all three types of wind conditions.

As Joe has already said, patterning is a balanced combination of instinct, training, and field experience. Well-bred hunting dogs, like their brethren wolves and coyotes, naturally use the wind to locate game. You must take advantage of that tendency by teaching your dog specific, controlled patterning styles, based on the proper use of wind.

Given the opportunity, you should always work your flushing dog into the wind (upwind). But you will have to use what nature offers on a hunt, whether that is an upwind, crosswind, or downwind situation. Even if you start out hunting into the wind, you can't continue to do so forever. And when you finish a piece of upwind cover, you will face crosswinds and/or following winds as you hunt back to your truck. A trained dog with several bird seasons under his collar will automatically run different patterns depending on wind conditions, but you must work with him to get to that point.

By itself, patterning teaches a pup only how to cover ground adequately relative to the wind. It does not guarantee that the dog will hunt within shotgun range, which is critical—above all else—for any flushing dog. A retriever or spaniel that runs perfect patterns at a hundred yards is better left at home to play with children and get fat. Hunting within gun range is a function of learned control and the dog's repeatedly finding birds at predetermined distances. You teach it along with patterning as a complete, drilled-in package so that you end up with a gun dog that is responsive to your demands, a flusher that hunts his ground thoroughly and within range, and a dog that makes game under whatever conditions exist.

Field of Dreams

Whenever possible, patterning drills should be carried out in fields designed for that purpose. I recommend the use of *groomed rows*. To create them, you must first determine the direction of the prevailing wind in your primary

Groomed rows are an excellent means of teaching your dog to pattern into the wind.

training field. Let's say, for example, that it blows mainly north to south. To develop a groomed field, mow at least ten five-yard-wide rows in the grass in an east-to-west direction. These cut rows should alternate with rows of grass left in its natural state. The mowed sections function as visual boundaries or lanes within which a young dog can run left and right, while the uncut rows let you plant birds that your dog cannot see. Because of the alternating cut and uncut rows, a field groomed in this fashion lets you train without assistants, if necessary, and at the same time develop a flushing dog that runs hard lines, makes sharp left and right casts, and consistently hunts in a more efficient, bird-producing pattern.

Throughout this chapter, my descriptions of upwind patterning drills are based on the use of a groomed field. However, don't give up hope if you don't have access to one—and I understand that many of you will not. By making a few adjustments, you can still follow this program and turn your pup into a competent hunter that runs good patterns. But before you abandon the idea of using a field with cut rows, do a little homework. Nearby bird-hunting and dog clubs may have such training grounds on their property.

Alternatively, if you know a local farmer with a field he doesn't intend to cut, you might be able to sweet-talk him into mowing rows for you. But, if you have ready access to a field with roughly ten- to twelve-inch-high grass but cannot arrange to have it groomed, you can run every drill described here simply by imagining that rows exist. Picture ten groomed rows and a centerline that cuts perpendicularly through them. For that matter, you can mark this centerline by placing stakes at each end of your field, and you can then use them as a beginning and end point when you work your dog downfield through the imaginary rows.

Here are two examples that might help: In the patterning instructions that follow (which are all based on the use of groomed rows), when I say, "Plant a pigeon twenty yards to the right in your first row," just put a bird twenty yards out, at a right angle to your starting point on the centerline. If I tell you, "Plant a bird twenty yards to the left in the second row," simply walk downfield ten to fifteen yards (that accounts for one cut and one uncut row), and plant your bird twenty yards to the left. Follow this same procedure through the ten imaginary groomed rows.

Your lack of actual mowed paths doesn't change how you should conduct any of the patterning drills that I present. Training in imaginary rows isn't quite as easy as using the real thing, but the concept will allow you to work readily through this chapter.

The Real Thing

Like my coauthor, I'm convinced that top upland flushing dogs are created by the use of birds—and plenty of them. For training purposes, "birds" usually refer to pigeons. In farm country, there is an endless supply that can be trapped around barns, silos, and livestock pens. Pigeons can also be raised at your home or, if you don't want that hassle, they can be purchased inexpensively from breeders who periodically cull their stocks of racers or homers.

If they are well cared for, then properly planted in a field, pigeons have a good flush, are strong fliers, and are extremely hardy birds that can serve repeatedly throughout several stages of training. The exceptions are clipwings, which can be used only as non-flyers until they molt or regrow trimmed or pulled flight feathers. Pigeons are a perfect size for young dogs to carry and are, as well, passive birds that won't beat up or frighten a youngster. In most states, pigeons are not protected by game laws, which means you can avoid the bureaucratic nightmare of licenses and permits required for training with legally designated game birds like chukars, Hungarian partridge, or pheasants.

From the very beginning of patterning work, I rely on live pigeons, rather than training dummies and/or dead birds. Although you can use these substitutes, some dogs do not respond well to them or, worse, quickly become bored by them. And, as Joe said earlier, a bored dog spells training trouble. All dogs benefit from—and some dogs re-quire—the excitement generated by the smell and motion of a live bird. I understand that people must use what they have within their individual circumstances, but do your ut-most to at least periodically spice up your dog's patterning drills with whatever live pigeons you can get. As a rule, one live bird is worth a truckload of canvas dummies.

However, if you are absolutely not in a position to maintain, trap, or purchase pigeons for the training pro-grams detailed in this chapter, don't despair. If dummies and/or dead birds are all you have available, substitute them for live pigeons in the drills I describe. But under-stand that they will not create flash, excitement, and drive in a young dog as readily as live birds.

A Bird in Hand

To help your dog learn patterning and other skills, you must know how to plant birds effectively, with a minimum of fuss. In Chapter 5's section on introducing a pup to gun-fire, Joe described the procedure for dizzying and planting pigeons to obtain a good flush and a strong flight.

Keep in mind that when we refer to flyers, we mean healthy birds with feathers intact, birds that flush and fly in a normal fashion. And, as Joe has explained, clipwings are birds with their flight feathers pulled, trimmed, secured with Velcro, or otherwise restrained so they can walk but not fly fast, far, or high. Lockwings have their wings interlaced behind their backs and cannot walk or fly; they stay where you plant them.

If you pattern-train without assistants, you will have to plant pigeons to aid in the process. Likewise, planted birds are required in the crosswind and downwind patterning drills I'll discuss later. If you're a novice handler training in a field without groomed rows, you can use six-inch strips of orange surveyor's tape—either placed on the ground or tied to a clump of grass—to help you remember precisely where your planted birds are. Normally, however, you should not mark bird locations because, over time, dogs learn that even a small piece of tape fluttering in the breeze means a bird is near.

More important, to place the tape you have to walk to a particular spot, which leaves the personal signature of your foot scent in a line straight to the bird. Retrievers and spaniels quickly learn to take the easy way out by following such foot scent. However, in these exercises it is important for the dog to locate all your planted pigeons, so use tape if you must. Just remember the drawbacks, and don't overdo it. Rubber-bottomed boots can reduce foot scent to some degree, but they can't eliminate its presence.

I generally plant a lock-wing or clip-wing pigeon by walking well off to the side of the point where I intend to locate the bird. I throw the pigeon ten yards or more into the field and away from where I walked, so there are no scent trails to the bird. (Obviously, there is no point in throwing a bird if you are using surveyor-tape site markings; you've already left a scent trail.) Don't worry about tossing the pigeon into your training field; you won't hurt it unless you rifle it in like a fastball.

Under most conditions, with most dogs, hand scent is not a serious issue. Minimal handling of birds usually does not create trouble. But don't fondle the pigeons; just take them from your bird bag and plant them. Contrary to the strong odor left by boots, low-level hand scent is overwhelmed by the smell of the bird. However, human smell can be a problem for a completely different reason: If your dog begins to avoid, or "blink," hand-scented birds it is usually because he associates the smell of your hand with punishment. This is a telltale symptom of the dog's confusion or your overly harsh training methods.

Outer Limits

Range refers to how far your dog is hunting in front of you and to your left and right. As we've said, a flushing dog must hunt and drive game birds into the air within reasonable shotgun range. If he is working and moving birds at distances beyond that, he is out of control and of no use to you—no matter how good he looks doing it. Put another way, the difference between a bird *hunter* and a bird *watcher* is often a matter of a few yards. Appropriate flushing-dog range is a matter of personal choice dictated mainly by the type of birds you're after, the kind of cover you hunt, and your skill with a shotgun. In training, your dog's range is established by the distance at which you plant training birds.

For example, if you are an average shotgunner who hunts a variety of birds in an array of covers, a good working range is roughly twenty yards to each side of you and fifteen yards in front of you. So, those are the distances at which you should plant training birds. But, if you are developing a tight-cover ruffed-grouse and woodcock dog, you will want your pup to run closer. In this case, you should plant your birds no more than fifteen yards to each side and ten yards in front. Conversely, if you want a bigger-running dog because you and several partners primarily hunt open-country birds like pheasants, or if you are an exceptional shot and can knock down birds at fifty-plus yards, then you can increase your dog's range by planting birds thirty yards to the left and right of the center path.

Either way, your dog will eventually become conditioned to run within the range that you establish by planting birds at that distance.

Keep in mind that it is easier to shorten a dog's range than to extend it. If, in the beginning, you start patterning work with your dog running thirty yards out on each side, it will be a simpler task to bring the dog into grouse range and run fifteen-yard patterns than it would be to take a dog that you trained with ten-yard right and left casts to become a wider-running pheasant dog.

Upwind Patterning

Because of your introductory training and its many repetitions, your dog should generally respond to "Sit" (or "Hup") and "Here," retrieve to hand, and turn on two whistle peeps. (I use the qualifier "generally " because this pup is not yet trained to obey with excellence.) These are prerequisites for serious pattern work. So is studying Figure 1, the upwind-patterning diagram on page 114; make certain that you understand it before proceeding

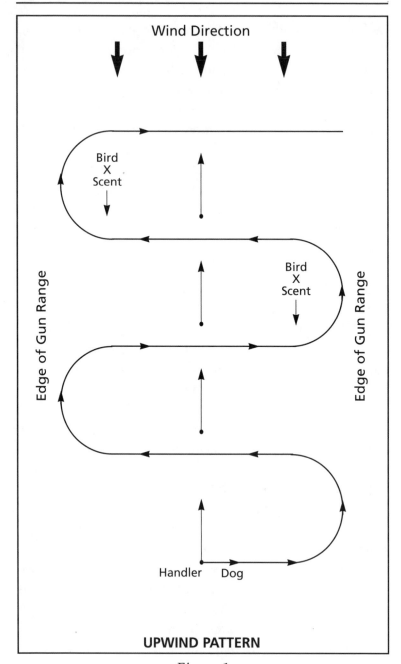

Figure 1

I use two different training methods to introduce the concept of quartering (upwind patterning). Although they aren't the only viable drills for this purpose, both work well for me.

For the strategy known as *teasing,* you will need two helpers—one on your left, the other on your right—each positioned at the same distance from you and your pup. (Note that the assistants should be in line with you, *not* in front of you or behind you.) Again, if you want a twenty-yard dog, these helpers should be about twenty yards on each side of you. Both should carry a lock-wing pigeon. Their job is to encourage the dog to run first to the left or right, then in the other direction, and so on.

Start by standing at one end of the field, near its center-line, and make sure that your dog will be running into the wind. Hold the pup by the collar or on lead until one of your helpers gets the dog's attention, shows him the bird, and "teases" him with it. (The other assistant should remain silent.) This first helper should call the dog's name, wave the bird, and shout "Pup! . . . Pup! . . . Pup! . . ." enthusiastically in a positive, nonthreatening manner. It is important that the teasers don't sound frustrated or angry, thereby giving your pup the impression that he is doing something wrong. Teasing is a confidence-building exercise and must be done in a upbeat fashion. Helpers should even play the fool (act silly) if that's necessary to grab the dog's attention.

At the sight and sound of the action, the dog should be jumping and pulling in his eagerness to go. After you release him and while your pup is running, the active teaser should throw the bird so that the dog can see him do it, tossing the lockwing five to eight yards out from his side. (Once he has thrown the bird, that helper must instantly stop any distracting activity.) Because the dog has already

While your pup is running, the active teaser throws his bird.
NOTE: *One of the teasers is out of the picture.*

been introduced to retrieving, he will run out, pick up the
bird, and bring it back to you. You then repeat this exercise
with the helper standing on the opposite side of the field.

This drill conveys to the dog the concept that he should
run outside (beyond) the teaser, who will eventually be re-
placed by a gunner, and not hunt short of him. Here again,
live birds are the stimulus, the motivating factor that will
make the dog want to run out there.

After you have repeated this exercise a few times and
your pup is consistently running outside the two helpers,
start moving rapidly down the field while the two assistants tease the dog back and forth. As you work your way
along, the teasers should stay in line with you, getting neither behind nor ahead of you. That's because you do not
want your dog to cut in back of you to reach the assistants,
and you do not want him to angle twenty yards out in front,

thereby failing to run a full left-to-right cast. When you stop, your teasers should stop; as you move forward, they should move forward. In the process, the groomed rows will keep your dog running a hard line to both sides of the field.

When your dog is running from left to right, the helper on the right-hand side should call the dog's name and tease him with the bird, using—as we've said—just about any motion to entice the dog toward him. This time, as the youngster approaches, the assistant must hide the bird behind his back. (Otherwise, the dog will remain at that helper's side, trying to get the bird, and that will break the animal's quartering momentum.) At the very moment the dog reaches the right-hand assistant, you—the handler— should give two beeps on the whistle while the helper on the left begins teasing, enticing the dog to reverse direction by shaking the bird, waving a hat, and excitedly calling the dog's name.

Because this is an advanced patterning drill, be sparing in your use of arm signals to turn the dog. Use them only when he needs your help. The goal is to develop a flusher that quests from side to side on his own, because in a hunting situation, you don't want to spend the day waving your arms around. Moreover, the extensive use of arm signals may encourage the dog to pop (wait for instructions from the handler before casting).

As you move down the field with the dog quartering back and forth between the teasers, have one of them throw a lockwing or clipwing five to eight yards ahead and to the side, *without allowing the dog to see it*. When your youngster takes a cast in that direction, he should smell the bird, pick it up, and deliver it to you. If he does not wind the pigeon, don't try to handle him to it. Forget it and keep moving.

The objective here is teaching the dog to pattern, not to find any particular bird. Don't let your pup become sidetracked from the drill by a long search for a pigeon. Get him moving and refocused with two peeps on your whistle while the helper on the other side teases, claps his hands, and calls your pup back across the training field.

While the dog was moving away from you, to either the right or left side, the opposite teaser should have thrown down a lockwing or clipwing five to eight yards in front and to the side so now that the dog is coming back down that row, he has another opportunity to smell a bird. You are motivating the dog to run from left to right by allowing him to smell birds on both sides of the field. Once the dog understands that there are never pigeons in the middle of the field, but only on the left and right, he will run from side to side because that pattern gets him birds.

Anytime your dog seems bored with the antics of the assistants, have a helper toss a lock-wing pigeon *so that the dog sees it*. This thrown bird is the right prescription for keeping the dog's interest level high. If you use a combination of lockwings that the dog sees and plants that he does not see—but finds while running toward a helper—his lightbulb will click on and he will get the idea that it is more rewarding to run a quartering pattern than to move straight down the field. I cannot tell you whether this breakthrough will occur after one session or a dozen. I *can* tell you that eventually the dog will learn to pattern left to right and right to left into the wind to seek game.

Always remember that your youngster is a creature of habit. He is going to use every available means that he has to find birds. If he can locate them more easily by using his eyesight, he'll do it. If he can find them more quickly by using your foot scent or by looking wherever you stop because it means that there is a planted bird there, he'll do it. By enlisting the help of teasers who move rapidly down the field, you are specifically conditioning your pup to run left and right and teaching him that only when he is runs that pattern, will he will find birds.

Although teasing can jump-start your dog's patterning and does help him understand the concept of quartering faster than all other methods, it is not a good idea to continue this exercise any longer than necessary. The reason is simple: When a helper throws a bird, it leaves scent and perhaps even feathers in the air. When the dog runs toward the teaser, he will smell that scent in the air and on the feathers that fell to the ground. The typical pup will start looking at that point, even though the actual bird is farther out. So, he may become confused and, not finding the bird right away, lose some confidence in his ability to smell. The second problem is that eventually your pup will spot a helper throwing a bird that the dog wasn't supposed to see. In all likelihood, he will then begin breaking his pattern and watching for a thrown bird instead of remaining focused on quartering down the field.

On Your Own

As already noted, many amateur trainers won't be able to find two cooperative helpers to throw birds for them during a succession of patterning drills. If you do not have two teasers, you can teach patterning on your own. (Understand that one teaser is a disadvantage; you must use two or none at all. If you have just one helper and he is on the left, the dog will learn only to run back and forth from you to that single teaser and will never venture to the other side of the training field.) I take advantage of two helpers when I have them, but I usually teach patterning alone.

If you are unable to enlist the help of teasers, you can jump-start your dog by walking him on lead as you plant birds. The last pigeon you put down will be the one the dog will find first, whereas the first one planted will be the last one he picks up. In other words, walk down the field with your dog, and plant a lockwing or clipwing at the end of the last row (we'll call it Row 6). It makes no difference if you plant the pigeon at the left- or right-hand end of the row. However, you do want to alternate ends in successive rows. For example, if you planted Row 6 on the left, plant Row 5 on the right, Row 4 on the left, and so on. Walk back to the centerline, and stand heading downfield. Sit your dog facing you, remove the lead, and hold the dog by his collar. Then release him with whatever voice command you have elected to use. (It makes no difference if you choose "Okay," "Hie on," or "Get out," but be consistent.)

The dog should remember the last plant and charge enthusiastically down the row. (I normally use lockwings in the beginning stages of teaching patterning, then vary the plants with clipwings and flyers as the dog begins to quarter more efficiently. Shooting a few flyers will spice up the drill for your dog. In any case, your pup should grab the birds eagerly and retrieve them for you.)

When your pup reaches the end of Row 1, give two peeps on the whistle and turn the dog in the opposite direction and into Row 2 where he will soon smell the plant at the end of that row. Repeat this procedure as you move down the field, with the dog finding birds on the right, then the left, then the right again.

Remember to always work your pup into the wind. Move rapidly in a zigzag pattern, encouraging him with, "Come on, let's go, let's go, thatta boy!" You want him to eagerly get out and run with you down the field. Each time you turn your dog, give two whistle peeps and clap your hands to cast him back to the other side until he has found the plants, or until you have finished working the field.

Once your dog has figured out the game, stop letting him see you plant the birds. Put down the pickups on alternating end of the rows when he is out of sight. By now, your pup should be quartering more efficiently and should find the birds without too much difficulty. Help him with his casts when necessary, but with more and more repetition, the dog should need less and less direction from you.

Moreover, because your pup will have found birds only at the sides of the field, not down the middle, he should begin to run aggressively out in front of you and to the left and right. For the rest of his life, his hunting world will not be at your side or behind you, and this basic drill helps to establish the correct pattern.

At this point, don't worry if the dog runs out of control and/or too far out. This will all fall into place as your pup develops, when the patterning becomes more formal and your demands for excellence and control escalate. Some dogs pick up the concept of this drill and the presence of birds after two or three sessions, while others may require fifteen or more sessions. The key to moving to the next and more formal stage of pattern training is when your dog clearly understands that when he comes to the training field, there are birds in front him. He should be excited about being cut loose and, by his actions, show you that he knows what he is supposed to do.

Don't expect your pup to succeed like a pro in the first training session. Remember, repetition is the key. Keep your early lessons short—about ten minutes apiece. As the dog grasps the concept, gradually increase the distance and number of left-to-right and right-to-left casts the dog makes between finds. Continue these drills until the dog quests for birds on his own, in a consistent quartering pattern.

Once you have your dog quartering and enthusiastically seeking birds, it is time to refine his first cast, which is critical, because it is the one that sets up patterning control, whether for field trialing or hunting. To build your pup's

A dog's first cast sets up his patterning style and his control.

excitement for the first cast, you should show him a planted lockwing. Walk the dog out with you when you plant the bird at the right-hand end of the first mowed row, then bring him back to its centerline and tell him to sit. Hold him firmly by the collar. He's not line steady at this point, so he can't be expected to stay put. Release him with your chosen voice command, and send him for the pigeon. He must understand the concept of the bird being out to the right.

Next, put the dog in his kennel, where he cannot see the action, and plant two birds in the first row, one approxi-

mately fifteen yards to the right of the centerline and another approximately fifteen yards to the left of the line.
Bring the dog to the centerline, and cast him to the right. If
he starts running down the center of the field, into the next
rows, bring him back and send him again. As was sug-
gested for earlier drills, you may have to help him by clap-
ping your hands, calling him, and walking toward the bird.
Use exaggerated arm and body motions so that he understands that he *must* run to the right. But don't show anger
or frustration; be upbeat.

Once he finds and delivers the bird on the right, bring
him back to the centerline and send him to the left. Again,
you will likely have to help him understand that you now
want him to move left. His instincts will tell him to run to
the right because that is where he found the last bird. After
a decent cast to the left and a successful retrieve, kennel the
dog for a ten- to fifteen-minute rest, then run this drill
again. You can repeat it three or four times during the
course of a day, but no more than that. As we have both said
before, you must avoid making the training process too ar-
duous and tedious.

You should run this drill until your dog understands
that there are *always* birds at *both* ends of the first row. Moreover, during this stage in your pup's education, the first-cast
drill is the only training you should work on each day. From
this point on, as long as the dog is aggressively hunting during patterning drills, you should be planting left and right
birds so that he always gets a bird *on his first cast,* regardless
of the direction. That won't happen in a real hunting situation, but if he thinks it will, he's going to set up properly and
run that first cast well. That, in turn, is going to put him in
position to run his second cast well, and if his second cast is
done properly, he will run a good third cast.

Once you have your dog running to the ends of the first row on his initial cast, you are ready to go to the next level of bird plants. Place a lockwing at either the left or right end of Row 1, at the range for which you are training. Next, put one at the opposite end of Row 2. Skip Row 3, then plant a bird in Row 4, at the end opposite the plant in Row 2. The purpose of skipping a row is to teach the dog to continue quartering even though he may not find a bird on every cast.

Set up on the centerline of the first row, and cast your dog to the end with the planted bird. Allow him to find the lockwing and make the retrieve. Now move forward, into row two, and send him in the opposite direction to find and pick up the bird. Continue down the field, casting him through Row 3 (which is "empty") and into Row 4, moving the dog in the opposite direction from the one he ran in Row 2. Start increasing the number of rows that remain empty, so that your dog has to hunt a little bit longer each time before finding a bird. But if he shows signs of confusion, go back to planting a pigeon at the end of every row. The point is to motivate your youngster to keep hunting hard in a quartering pattern.

Crosswind Patterning

As shown in Figures 2 and 3, a crosswind pattern is run in a zigzag fashion with the handler sending the dog downwind on the first cast so that he makes a big loop before cutting back into the wind on the diagonal.

In developing a crosswind pattern, you should *not* rely on teasers or groomed rows, which are used only to start your dog quartering into the wind. (The same is true of downwind patterning.) A field with ten- to twelve-inch-high grass is ideal. If the crosswind is blowing from left to

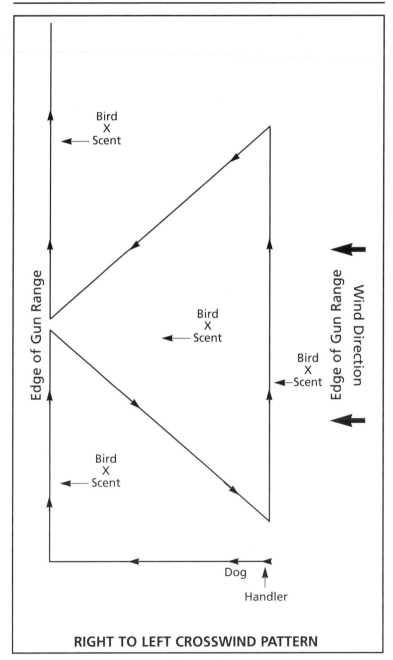

Figure 2

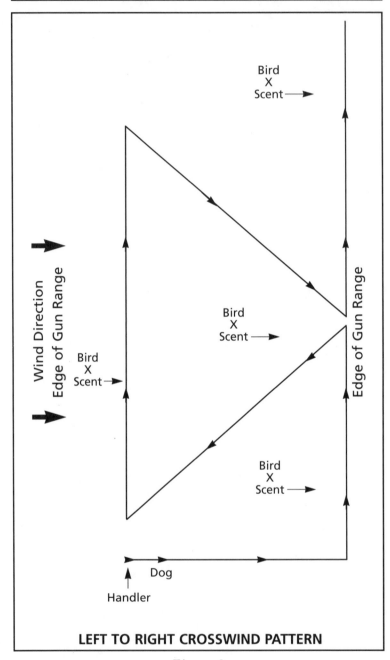

LEFT TO RIGHT CROSSWIND PATTERN

Figure 3

right, plant a pigeon about fifteen yards to the right of the centerline. Cast your dog from the centerline in the direction of the planted bird. By now he should be screaming down the row to find the pot of gold at the end of the rainbow—the bird.

The difference between this drill and the upwind drill is that your dog must be *beyond* the bird in order to body-scent it. As in all patterning exercises, we are trying to teach the dog to put himself in the best possible position to scent the bird, yet remain in gun range. If the dog ran a quartering pattern in a crosswind or downwind situation, he would not be maximizing his chances of locating his quarry by body-scenting. Instead, he would likely push running birds, such as pheasants, ahead of him. This would put your flusher in the position of having to track the bird by taking foot scent, which makes putting a bird in the bag much tougher.

Let's return to the training field. Once the dog is readily finding and retrieving your initial plant by casting downwind, it is time to move ahead. (Due to the repetition accomplished in your upwind drills, this should take no time at all.) Now, put the dog away so that he can't see you, and make your first plant fifteen or so yards to the right of the centerline *and five yards up the field.*

As before, starting on the centerline, cast your pup downwind (to the right in this case). When he gets out around the fifteen-yard mark, he will expect to find a bird because he always has. When he discovers that it's not there, odds are he will naturally move forward the five yards to where your plant is. If he starts to come back to you, move up the field yourself, calling the dog's name or whistling to get his attention. If necessary, help him find the plant.

If at all possible, repeat this drill a couple of times daily over as many days as it takes for the dog to get the hang of running the downwind cast and then moving up the field the five yards or so to find the bird. Every once in a while, plant a lockwing or clipwing on the imaginary line he runs before cutting upfield. This will help to keep him honest and taking the fifteen-yard cast to the left or right (depending on the direction of the crosswind).

Once the dog is reliable in this exercise, plant one pigeon fifteen yards along the downwind cast and a second bird at approximate right angles to the line of the cast, *ten* yards upfield. When you cast your dog downwind, he should quickly find your first plant and retrieve it. Now cast him again downwind. As he runs the fifteen yards, you should be moving forward, up the centerline. Your pup will probably turn and cut up field, too. If he does not, get his attention and move him forward so that he finds and retrieves the second plant. Remember, this bird is only five yards farther upfield than it was in the initial crosswind drills. The key is to advance in small increments.

When the dog is consistently finding and retrieving both the first plant (fifteen yards down the imaginary row) and the second plant (ten yards upfield) *without your moving from your original spot*, put down your second pigeon fifteen yards out (instead of ten). Again, though, make a first plant fifteen yards downwind, on the line of the cast. When your dog is accomplished at finding and retrieving both of these birds (once more, without your moving forward or otherwise assisting him), make your second plant *twenty* yards down the field.

Essentially, you can structure these drills to create a crosswind patterning habit that suits your hunting style. If you want a dog that runs fifteen yards downwind, then moves upfield twenty yards when he's pursuing game birds, make your plants accordingly whenever you train him on crosswind patterns. If you're looking for something different, place the two pigeons so as to establish the style of quartering you are looking for.

Once your dog consistently runs the pattern you want, you are now ready to work on the diagonal cut-back cast, as shown in Figures 2 and 3. First, put a bird fifteen yards downwind, but do *not* plant a second one farther downfield of that point. Cast your dog for the pigeon. Once he has retrieved it, cast him downwind again. He should run out the fifteen yards and, upon not finding a bird, should continue up the field at a right angle to the wind, as he has previously learned to do. While he is running downwind and away from you, toss a lock-wing pigeon about five yards in front of you. Do *not* let him see you throw this bird.

When the dog gets up the field twenty yards—to the spot where he previously found the second plant, call his name, say "Here," clap your hands, and get him to come back to you. Be upbeat and enthusiastic. When he gets to within five yards of you, he should smell the lockwing you tossed. Alternate this drill with the exercise where you plant one bird on the line of the downwind cast and a second bird twenty yards farther upfield. Otherwise the dog will decide there is no need to run up the field.

Soon, with plenty of repetition, your flusher will master the pattern that has him running downwind for fifteen yards, moving up the field for twenty, then running a diagonal back toward you. Now you need to get him to cast back *into the wind.*

Make your usual plant fifteen yards downwind, but do *not* put down a second upfield pickup as before, and do *not* toss a lockwing in front of you. Instead, plant a bird about fifteen yards out on your *upwind* side and ten to fifteen yards upfield. (Note this is the side opposite the one to

which you will initially cast the dog.) Once your pup has retrieved the first plant, cast him downwind again. He should
run out fifteen yards and then move up the field twenty.
When he reaches the point where he has picked up a bird in
past drills, call him back toward you. As he runs in, cast
him to the upwind side by giving him an arm signal, extending your arm straight out, parallel to the ground, and
pointing it in the direction you want the dog to move. You
may have to jog upwind to encourage him, but the breeze
will be blowing the scent of the bird in his direction, and
bang—he should smell it and head for it.

By judiciously making your plants downwind, upfield
on the downwind side, in front of you, or on the upwind
side, you can create a crosswind pattern that your dog will
start to run as a habit. The key is to plant with a purpose,
putting down birds so that your dog will run the pattern *because it works for him*. As a result, you will not have to yell
and repeatedly blow your whistle as you try to handle the
dog.

Once you can get your flusher to run the downwind
cast, cut upfield, run a diagonal back to you, then cast into
the wind, the rest is relatively easy. As you move down the
field, continue to toss lockwings in front of you for the
dog's diagonal cutback—not on every cast, but often
enough so the dog learns, "Hey, birds are also near The
Boss. I better check there too and not just run straight
downfield."

Downwind Patterning

In order for your pup's olfactory powers to fulfill their
potential, the wind must be moving from the bird to the
dog's nose. Thus, in a downwind situation, where the wind

is blowing from behind you to the pigeon that's planted in front, the dog must be *beyond* the bird in order to wind it. In other words, if the dog works downwind, he will bump the pigeon before he can smell it.

The most productive downwind pattern is a figure eight (see Figure 4). To establish it, you're going to plant some birds (flyers, clipwings, or lockwings) in the middle of your training field, in addition to putting down pigeons on the left and right sides of the centerline, at the outer edge of the range that you want your dog to run.

For your first cast, with the wind at your back, plant a bird at right angles to your forward path down the centerline, at the desired distance. (We used fifteen yards in our crosswind drills, so I will stick with that for this example, but the choice of range is yours.) In a downwind drill, it makes no difference whether this plant—and, therefore, your first cast—is to the left or right. Plant a second bird in the middle of the field, approximately ten to fifteen yards in front of you.

Cast your dog to the side where you made your first plant. He should find and retrieve this bird. Now cast him to either side. He should run out the fifteen yards and then cut up field, just as he did in the crosswind drill. When he gets twenty yards out, give him two peeps on the whistle, call his name, clap your hands, and *run to the side away from him* in order to get him to change direction and move across the field. As he responds, he should smell your second plant in the middle of the field and retrieve it. By continuing to plant birds to the left and right at a fixed distance, you will establish your dog's outer range and imprint it on his brain. And, by mixing in the shorter centerline plants, you will create a downwind pattern in which he won't hunt too deep.

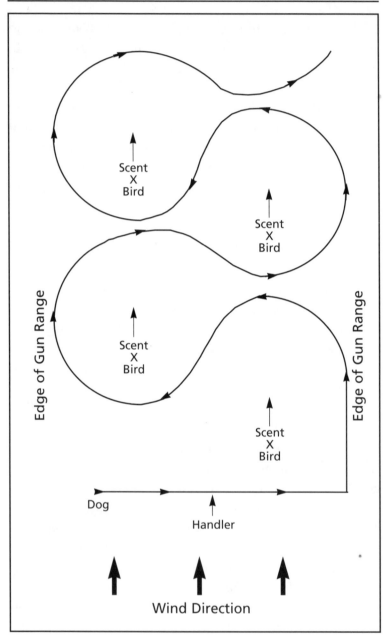

Scent
X
Bird

Scent
X
Bird

Scent
X
Bird

Edge of Gun Range

Scent
X
Bird

Edge of Gun Range

Dog

Handler

Wind Direction

Figure 4

Because they soon learn that they have to be beyond the bird in order to scent it, many flushers have a tendency to run big in a downwind situation. For that reason, it is often beneficial to stop planting pigeons downfield after you put down a bird for the dog's first left and/or right cast. Instead, carry a few clipwings or lockwings in your vest or bird bag. When the dog is running his pattern—and not looking at you—roll in (toss) a pigeon five yards in front of you as you are moving down the centerline. Call the dog back toward you by voice or a whistle. As he approaches you, he will find the bird and—with repetition—will develop a habit of looping back into the wind instead of bolting too far downfield.

As in other patterning drills, you can speed up the initial learning process by using arm signals for casts and changes of direction. However, I drop these as patterning progresses. I prefer whistle commands for a finished flusher, because in hunting situations, the dog often cannot see me. Moreover, constantly waving your arms while carrying a shotgun can make for a long day.

In the Final Analysis

Patterning will often break down when you're hunting in the woods or fields, where there are natural obstructions, manmade barriers (like fences), and shifting winds. But if you initially establish solid patterning routines, your dog will retain them throughout his life, and they will make him far more effective in using the wind to find game. They will also condition your flusher to hunt within gun range, underscoring the fact that patterning and range go hand in hand.

Every training drill is a building block that goes into creating a strong foundation on which, in turn, you can build a finished product. Throughout this chapter, I have described habit-forming methods based on repetition and a gun dog's single, most powerful motivating factor—live birds. A talented dog with drive wants birds more than anything else you can offer, and if he finds them by running particular patterns at certain distances, that is how he will always run.

And it is an undeniable fact that a retriever or spaniel trained to pattern effectively—within shotgun range, under any wind conditions—will *always* find more birds than an untrained or randomly running dog.

7.

Refining Basic Commands— Demanding Excellence

The objective at this stage of the program is to teach your dog to obey *the first time* you give a command. Because you are beginning formal training, you must require obedience, whereas up to now you have been simply showing the pup what you expect. From this point on, you should issue a command once and correct your youngster for disobedience, as well as praising (rewarding) him for obedience.

Before you enter the formal training stage, which begins with drilling the dog in the four primary yard commands, it is imperative that your youngster understand the meaning of each one. That was the purpose of the "Show Pup" stage. By now, you should have done hundreds of "Show Pups" for each of the four commands that Joe Arnette described in Chapter 5. They are: "Kennel," which involves your dog going away from you; 2) "Sit" (or "Hup"), which means that your dog sits and stays put; "Here" (or "Come"), which is the recall command; and "Heel," where your dog walks at your side.

Before you can successfully complete formal training, you need to review several points that Joe presented earlier. First, dogs are place oriented. In other words, correction for disobedience or reward for obedience must take place where a specific action occurred. Second, dogs are also time oriented. If your pup doesn't come when you tell him "Here" but you wait five minutes to discipline him, he will not associate the correction with his earlier disobedience. Rather, he will more likely associate the punishment with whatever he was doing at the moment of discipline and with his location at the time the correction is delivered.

Again, your standards must be more stringent at this turning point in the training program. If you say "Here" one time, your dog should immediately come to you. If you say "Sit" or "Hup," your dog should drop when you give the command. His reaction to the stimulus of your command must become a habit. This is the *conditioned response* that Joe presented in Chapter 4, and that is what you are training to achieve. At the end of his formal training in yard commands, your dog should immediately obey *because he has been conditioned to do so*. His trained, appropriate response to your instructions has to become an instantaneous, nonthinking reaction.

There are two dominant forms of this process. One is *classical conditioning,* which Russian physiologist Ivan Pavlov made famous. He rang a bell, then immediately fed a subject dog. After enough repetitions, the dog paired the ringing with the feeding and began salivating immediately upon hearing the bell.

Operant conditioning is behavior modification evoked by the use of rewards for appropriate responses (positive reinforcement). This theory reflects the principle that the association between a stimulus and response is strengthened when the response is followed by positive reinforcement. Training your dog to respond to your commands (whether given verbally or with the whistle) the first time you deliver them involves both classical *and* operant conditioning.

To refresh your memory, each of the yard commands ("Kennel," "Sit," "Here," and "Heel") involves four stages of learning:

1. Show Pup (which you have already completed)
2. Stimulus-Command-Response
3. Command-Stimulus-Response
4. Command-Response

Keep in mind that at this point in the program, once you have advanced to a particular stage in training a command, you should never retreat to a previous level. For example, when you begin "Command-Stimulus-Response," do not move back to "Stimulus-Command-Response" or "Show Pup" for that specific command. You should remain in "Command-Stimulus-Response" as long as necessary, then move on to "Command-Response." Remember, too, that it is a mistake to correct a dog for disobedience on one occasion but not discipline him for the same infraction at another time. You must be consistent if you are going to create conditioned responses.

The Get-In Command

You should commence formal training with "Kennel." You are going to *teach* (as opposed to *show*) your pup that he must obey your command the first time you give it. He will learn that he can "turn off" stimulation (in the form of physical pressure) in the "Stimulus-Command-Response" stage and that he can avoid stimulation altogether by obeying in the "Command-Stimulus-Response" stage. Also, you will further advance the safe-zone concept that was introduced in Chapter 4.

There is a major advantage to using electronic stimulation in teaching the yard commands (see Appendix B—*Introduction to Training With Electronics*). With that in mind—and to reduce confusion—I have used electronic-training terminology such as "stimulus" and "stimulation" throughout this chapter. Whether you apply pressure with a slip lead or electronic stimulation with an E-collar, the concept is the same.

In the "Stimulus-Command-Response" phase you will apply the stimulus first, then give the command. The pressure should be continuous, not sporadic or momentary, and it should be maintained until your dog responds with the desired behavior. The disadvantage of momentary stimulation is that the dog has more difficulty understanding that a specific response on his part caused that stimulus to end. He may associate what he was doing at the exact moment the stimulus ceased as the reason the stimulus ended. Thus, if he was fighting going into the kennel when the stimulus stopped, he might actually learn to fight harder to stay out of it the next time around.

When teaching the "Kennel" command, you can apply continuous stimulation by using a self-tightening slip lead. Place it over your dog's head so that the loop is just above his ear on the side farthest from you and around his neck on the side closest to you. Any cord, lead, or rope will suffice, as long as you can apply continuous pressure on the point just above the dog's outside ear, pressure that will cease when you release the tension on the cord.

The proper position for the self-tightening slip lead.

Start off standing within six to eight feet of the kennel, with the dog on your left side (if that's where you did the "Show Pup" for "Heel"). First, administer the stimulus (pull steadily on the cord), then say "Kennel." Remember, *say it only once*; commands are repeated only in the "Show Pup" stage. At first, however, you may have to push the dog into the kennel while applying ear pressure. When your pup goes in, instantly release the tension on the cord, and alleviate the pressure at the point of contact just above the dog's ear. Keep repeating this exercise until your youngster starts to go into the kennel immediately upon feeling the ear pressure—even before you give the command "Kennel." When that happens, you'll know he understands how to turn off the stimulus of ear pressure. Note that once your dog has figured this out, it is *much* easier to later teach him that he can avoid the stimulation altogether by obeying your command the first time you give it.

As with all training, keep the sessions short. Numerous five-minute lessons will create a much more responsive and happy pup than will grueling half-hour struggles. It is not important that your dog grasp the concept in the first few minutes or even on the first day. Eventually, he will perceive the kennel as a safe zone because when he is in it there is no pressure on his ear.

In this early stage, it makes no difference if he remains in the kennel or comes out. Later, you can demand that your dog stay in the kennel until you give him a release command, such as "Okay," whereby he leaves the kennel and comes to you. But that is down the road. If your youngster wants to stay inside the kennel, use the opportunity to get in a few "Show Pups" by repeating "Here . . . Here . . . Here" as you pull him to you. Remember, going back to this basic stage is fine for a command that you haven't yet begun to refine.

Once you are certain that your dog knows how to turn off the pressure by going into the kennel, it is time to move on to "Command-Stimulus-Response," where the order of things is reversed. There is no advantage to staying at the previous level any longer than necessary.

Here, as before, start six to eight feet from the kennel. Give the command first—again, saying it just once—then apply the stimulus (ear pressure) if your dog does not immediately go into the kennel, and keep it on until he complies. As soon as he enters the kennel, release the ear pressure. Again, keep the sessions short.

With enough repetition, your dog will progress toward the "Command-Response" stage. He will learn that he can avoid the pressure by obeying with your command immediately. He will come to understand that running away, sulking, and struggling do not work for him but that obeying your very first command solves his problem. Moreover, in time your dog's response will become habit—a *conditioned* response to a particular command. As a result, he will respond correctly every time you issue that command.

The Cornerstone: "Sit"

As with the "Kennel" command, your dog should understand *exactly* what "Sit" or "Hup" means before you leave "Show Pup" and progress to "Stimulus-Command-Response." Again, in this stage, you give the command once and only once.

Walk your dog (on lead) onto the training board discussed in Chapter 5, push his rear end down, and say "Sit" (or "Hup"). You are now teaching the dog that he is to sit on the command the first time you give it. Because of all your work with "Show Pups" on the board, he will anticipate that he is to sit and will likely do so as soon as he walks onto the board. (Indeed, the advantage of numerous "Show Pups" is that your dog will not be in the "Stimulus-Command-Response" stage very long.)

Your dog should sit automatically when he feels your hand pushing him down on the board.

As soon as he sits immediately upon walking onto the board or feeling the stimulus of your pushing his rear down, you are ready to move on to "Command-Stimulus-Response." Walk your dog onto the board and say "Sit." If he does not obey, correct him with continuous pressure by pushing his butt down more forcefully and holding it down. Once he's sitting, you should be able to walk away. If he comes off the board, do not give the command again, because if he sits, you will then have to praise him when he was actually a bad boy by not staying put the first time around. Instead, pick him up, put him back on the board, and push his rear end down.

When I say to "pick up your dog," I mean that literally. Even if your youngster is a large retriever, do your best to get him off the ground and back onto the board under your control. (In carrying out this correction, don't be emotional, and don't coddle the dog enroute.) It is much easier for a dog to understand why he is being corrected if he is carried. By not picking him up, you risk his thinking that he is being punished away from the board for some transgression he doesn't know he committed.

Continue these drills until your dog is religious in his response to "Sit." By "religious," I mean that when you walk him onto the board and tell him to sit, he obeys and stays put. As with the "Kennel" command, you should then release the dog from his sitting position with an "Okay" or "All right." Your choice of words is not important, but consistency is. Don't use "Okay," as a release command one time, then shift to "Let's go" (or something similar) the next. If your pup is reluctant to release from "Sit," encourage him with an enthusiastic tap on the shoulder or a tug on his collar.

Now walk him on a lead or check cord and say "Sit." Expect the dog to obey in the exact spot where he was when you gave the command. If he moves, pick him up, return him to that point, and make him sit with hand pressure. Treat wherever he was when you gave the command "Sit" as if it were on an imaginary board.

Then, with the dog *away* from your side, but still on a long lead or check cord, say "Sit" once. When he obeys in the exact location where he was standing when you issued the command, walk out and praise him. If he fails to obey, pick him up and put him back on that spot, again making him sit with hand pressure. Once more, your dog must learn that you want an appropriate response to the command the *first* time you give it—not the fourth or fifth or twelfth time. As soon as you say "Sit," he must obey immediately. Once he is responding consistently, though, you can begin teaching him to sit on whistle commands and hand signals.

This process involves the principles of what I refer to as "pre-cue/cue." The cue, which in this case is your voice command, has already been taught: When you say "Sit," the dog obeys. Therefore, if you give one peep on the whistle (the pre-cue) followed immediately by the verbal command "Sit" (the cue), the pre-cue will eventually prompt the same response as the cue. You will no longer need to issue the verbal command. Follow through with the same drill I described for teaching "Sit" via voice, using the concept of an imaginary board. Then advance to walking your dog on lead, giving a peep on the whistle, and immediately delivering the verbal command "Sit." As always, remember to praise your dog when he performs well, and take him back to the point of any failure to obey during a correction. Do peep–"Sit". . . peep–"Sit". . . peep–"Sit" repetitions until the dog anticipates that you are going to say "Sit" immediately after giving a peep on the whistle. At this point, the whistle command is evoking the same response as the voice command, and you can drop the latter.

You will use the pre-cue/cue concept throughout much of your training, such as when you are asking your dog to be steady to the flush, the shot, or a "volunteer" bird, and when you want him to sit down during a blind retrieve at your whistle or voice signal. Indeed, once a foundation command—in this case "Sit"—has been instilled in your pup, all future "association" commands will be taught with the pre-cue/cue system. Taught in this manner, the "Sit" command is the mortar that will cement all the advanced building blocks. That is why it is imperative your dog obey the very first time. This point will become even clearer as you gradually expand the distance at which you expect him to sit upon hearing either the whistle or the voice command.

For upland hunters, the hand signal for "Sit" is one of the *least* important commands. It requires that the dog be facing you, and in this position he is not questing for game. Think of the hand signal as a reinforcement of the verbal or whistle "Sit" command, with its major purpose being to serve as an aid during blind retrieves. Still, although it is far more important for an upland flusher to sit on the voice, whistle, flush, and shot than on a hand command, your dog must understand what a raised hand means.

To train him to sit on a hand signal, again use the pre-cue/cue approach. First, put your pup on a lead or check cord, and wait until he is in front of you and looking your way. If you raise your hand (the pre-cue) and immediately follow up with the command (the cue) he knows so well, the dog will soon anticipate that the command "Sit" follows the hand signal.

Once your pup clearly understands that the manual signal means "Sit," drop the verbal command. Simply raise your hand over your head. If the dog does not sit, give a sharp upward snap on the lead while pushing his rear to the ground. Do not repeat the command. Each time your pup *does* respond to the hand signal properly, give him a quick pat and an "Attaboy." Eventually, he won't have to think about obeying; his reaction will be automatic.

Total Recall: Teaching "Here"

Formal training of "Here" is simple if you've completed the "Show Pup" stage and your dog absolutely understands the meaning of the command. When you move to "Stimulus-Command-Response," put a check cord on him, and pull on it as you give the command "Here." Then, when the dog gets to you, release the pressure. With enough repetitions, your pup will begin to move toward you when he feels the pull of the check cord—*before* the verbal command is issued. Once he starts coming, slack the line; very quickly, he will learn to turn off the stimulus by coming to you. When your dog understands what he can accomplish by obeying, it will be much easier for him to learn to avoid pressure in the "Command-Stimulus-Response" stage.

In this phase of the program, say "Here" and—if he does not respond—pull on the check cord. Don't jerk it; just apply steady pressure. Remember, you want the stimulation to be continuous, not momentary. Once the dog starts coming to you, take the tension off; if he stops, resume pulling on the cord. Very soon, when you say "Here," you will not have to pull on the check cord. The dog will respond to the command alone.

Now shift your training to a confined area—a fenced yard, a garage, or a basement. For this exercise, leave the check cord on the dog, but do not hold on to it. When he is running in the confined area, say "Here" and if he does not come, grab the check cord and pull him to the spot where you were standing when you issued the command. (Do not, however, repeat the command.) Whenever you say "Here" and your dog obeys, praise him. This is a key command, and you want him to enjoy obeying it.

It is imperative that you never correct your pup when

he comes to you. Look at it this way: Suppose you say "Here" and the dog does not obey, but instead runs around while you shout the command. Eventually, however, he does come. Now if you correct him, he will associate the correction with the act of coming to you. This is worse than counterproductive; it may teach your dog not to come back.

An even more compelling reason to avoid this correction is that you, the handler, will no longer be a safe zone. Remember, up to this point, you have essentially taught the dog that when you give the command "Here" and he responds by coming to your side, he is completely safe. Therefore, he learns that it is in his best interest to obey. (The concept of the safe zone and its relationship to the command "Here" is dealt with extensively in Appendix B— *Introduction to Training With Electronics.*)

To teach your dog to come on the whistle, again use the concept of pre-cue/cue. First, with your dog on a check cord, give him the recall command (I prefer a continuous trill, though others use four sharp, distinct peeps), immediately followed by the voice command "Here." The whistle is the pre-cue; the verbal command is the cue. If the dog does not obey, don't issue either the verbal or whistle command again. If he has moved at all, pick him up and return him to the point of disobedience, then pull him to you with the check cord. With enough repetitions, the whistle will evoke the same response as the voice.

You can now train without the voice and use just the whistle. If you give the whistle command alone and the dog does not come, again pull him to you using the check cord. Conversely, when your flusher responds immediately, let him know that he was a good boy. Again, you're using the principles of classical and operant conditioning—via repetition—to create a conditioned response.

Stand by Your Man: "Heel"

As with "Kennel," "Sit," and "Here," the prelude to formally training the "Heel" command involves many "Show Pups." Then, to begin "Stimulus-Command-Response," place a slip lead over your dog's head (you can also use a pinch or choke collar, but I prefer the lead). Leave the left side of the lead's loop just over the dog's left ear if you are teaching him to heel on the left, reversing its position if you want your hunting partner on your right side.

As Joe mentioned earlier, if you are right-handed, you probably carry your shotgun with your right hand. Thus, it will be more convenient if your dog heels on the left. By contrast, if you are left-handed, you may want him on the right. It's up to you. Either way, the loop should be just above the ear farthest from you as you start walking. Whenever the dog is forging ahead or lagging behind, apply continuous stimulation by pulling him back to your knee. Immediately after you start apply pressure, command "Heel" *once*. The moment the dog is back by your knee, release the tension on the lead. Eventually, he will come to the heel position upon feeling the pressure over his ear—even before you give the command. Once you are certain that he knows how to turn off the stimulus (ear pressure) by heeling, advance to the "Command-Stimulus-Response" stage.

Start by walking your dog on lead and issuing the command "Heel." If he lunges forward, pull him (but don't jerk him) back to your knee. Again, the idea is to keep continuous stimulation (ear pressure) on him until he is back in place. With sufficient repetition, your dog will learn that he experiences no discomfort when he is at your knee but receives correction when he is not. Thus, your knee becomes a safe zone. When you command "Heel" and the dog obeys both immediately and consistently, he has arrived at the desired point—"Command-Response."

Before moving to even more advanced training, you should remember that the "Stimulus-Command-Response" stage is part of the training program *only for yard commands.* Virtually all additional commands will be taught using the concept of pre-cue/cue. In the future, you will show your dog what you want, then move directly to "Command-Stimulus-Response," and end with "Command-Response."

Part Three: Postgraduate Work— Advanced Training

8.

Steadiness to Flush and Shot

A flushing dog cannot be considered "finished," or fully trained, unless he is steady, though some hunters believe that at the flush, the dog should be in hot pursuit of the flying bird. That way, they argue, when the bird is shot the flusher will get to the mark more quickly, thus having a better chance of retrieving a crippled bird. I strongly disagree with this philosophy.

A dog that is sitting at the flush and concentrating on marking the fall will get to the bird more quickly than a dog in uncontrolled pursuit. For example, let's say a bird flushes while a dog is trailing it through high grass. Once airborne, the bird hooks to the right and is shot. Because the dog is in full chase through tall cover, he won't see the bird veer or fall, and he will continue downfield on its original line of flight. Because he was unsteady, this dog can't perform what should have been a simple pickup and will be forced into a blind retrieve or no retrieve at all. He may also flush other game—out of gun range—

while pursuing the bird in the wrong area.

An even more compelling argument for steadiness involves safety. If, for example, you or a partner shoot while the dog is in hot pursuit of a low-flying bird, and if at that moment your pup makes a sudden jump for the bird, you risk injuring him—or worse. Trouble can come in yet another fashion: If you are hunting with a partner—and if his flusher is also unsteady—each dog will each believe that a given retrieve is his, and a fight could ensue.

By definition, a steady flushing dog is under control and hunting within gun range. As such, he will always put more birds in the bag than a flusher that is not steady. Most often, hunters who argue against steadying to flush and shot own dogs that are seldom in control.

In this chapter, I will cover steadying your retriever or spaniel to flush and shot through the use of traditional methods. (Again, electronic training is addressed in Appendix A.) During this stage of training, there cannot be long lapses between sessions, so don't start to steady your dog one day and then go on vacation for two weeks. Choose a block of time that you can commit fully to the steadiness program.

At this point, your dog has been introduced to birds, has learned to pattern, has been introduced to the gun, and is retrieving to hand. He has also been trained to come on a voice or whistle command and to respond reliably to "Sit." Most important, he has had months of actively flushing and chasing birds. As Joe Arnette told you in his introduction, many British trainers do not encourage flushing and chasing prior to teaching steadiness, believing it creates a dog that is, at best, difficult to control and, at worst, completely out of control. I take exception to this. I believe that a dog that has been allowed to flush and chase before being steadied is bolder, more competent, and more confident around birds. As a result, he is much less likely to develop problems with gun-shyness, retrieving, or flushing.

In field trials, a hesitant flush is usually a one-way ticket home. But a weak flush is also a problem in the real world of upland bird hunting. The last thing some wild birds want to do is fly; they would rather escape on the ground. And the more time you give those birds to run, the greater the likelihood they will get away. Remember, in the wild you are hunting birds that predators have not been able to kill. You want to make sure that your dog has an aggressive flush that will put those birds into the air quickly.

Steadiness is completely unnatural to the flushing/retrieving breeds; that is, there is no genetic basis for them to be steady to flush and shot. Everything in our dogs' brains says that they should chase a flushed bird as far as they can see it. Now, however, we are going to demand that on the flush, they hit the ground and sit, then wait to hear their names called for a retrieve.

Preparation for Steadiness to Shot

For the initial stages of this process, I recommend a .22 training pistol or a .410 shotgun. You can conduct these exercises anyplace that is free of distractions and where gunfire is not an issue.

With your dog walking next to you *on lead*, fire the gun into the air, then immediately give the "Sit" command, either verbally or by whistle: BANG!—"Sit." As always, when introducing commands (you should now consider the shot to be a new command), the one your dog already knows should be given last. In this case, "Sit" should always follow the shot, not the reverse. (Remember the pre-cue/cue concept introduced in the previous chapter.)

After a number of repetitions of firing the gun and commanding "Sit," the dog will associate the sound of the shot with the command that follows and soon will sit at the shot. Ultimately, the sound of the shot will elicit the same response as the original command. When your dog has made the association to sit upon hearing the shot (pre-cue), drop the follow-up command (cue). You will know the dog has made the connection when he begins to sit after the shot, but before you give the verbal or whistle command.

At this point, if your pup does not sit when you fire a shot, don't give the verbal or whistle command. You are teaching the dog to sit immediately upon hearing the shot—no excuses. Simply pick up the dog, return him to the spot where he was when the shot went off, and firmly push his rear down while holding his collar to keep his head up. Once he is sitting, let him know that's what you wanted by giving him a pat or an "Attaboy." Do not overdo the praise—or the correction. Again, repetition is the key to creating a conditioned response. By repeating this exercise often enough, by administering correction at the point of disobedience, and by drilling-in the command with positive reinforcement, your dog will put his butt down at a shot without even thinking.

Once your flusher is consistently sitting to shot on lead, let him run around dragging a check cord during your training sessions. Fire a shot, but do not give a verbal or whistle command. If the dog sits immediately, walk out and praise him. If he does not obey, pick him up and return him to where he was when the shot went off. Make him sit without a verbal/whistle command, using hand and collar pressure. Continue with this drill until his response is absolutely reliable.

In the early stages of teaching steadiness to shot, always

walk all the way to your dog after he sits. If you immediately release him by commanding "Here" after he puts his rear on the ground, he will think that he is supposed to come to you instead of staying where he is. Moreover, if you always say "Here" after he has been sitting for three seconds, he will eventually start returning to your side *with no command* after sitting for precisely that length of time.

As you advance in your steadiness-to-shot training, adopt the following procedure: When the shot is fired and the dog responds by sitting, vary the manner in which you release him. Walk toward him each time but stop at a different distance before you say "Here." In addition, don't always give the command immediately; make him wait for different lengths of time. You want your flusher to remain sitting after the shot, no matter how long it may be before he is released. Again, it is important that he not think that he is to run back to the handler after briefly sitting on the shot. In an actual hunting situation, the dog would be commanded either to retrieve fallen game or to continue hunting if the bird were missed. Very seldom would it be more efficient for your pup to return to your side.

Line Steadiness

The concept and necessity of line steadiness, where you command your dog to sit and he remains sitting until sent for a retrieve, are not difficult to grasp. In waterfowl and dove shooting, or on preserve-sponsored driven hunts, your dog should remain by your side and mark the birds that fall in front of you. In an upland situation, your dog will be hunting ahead of you, and at a flush he should sit and mark the bird's flight and fall. Thus, line steadiness is simply a prelude to having the dog steady to wing and shot. If you are unable to keep your dog steady at your side, it is unrealistic to expect him to sit when a cackling rooster flushes twenty yards away from you.

In an earlier chapter, Joe Arnette emphasized that you should not introduce line steadiness until just prior to teaching steadiness to flush and shot. Before this, your dog should be allowed to chase and flush and retrieve without the pressure of remaining steady. Training line steadiness should not take a long period of time, but it is important that your dog perform with total reliability before you move on to the next step in the program.

When you begin to teach line steadiness, put a check cord on your dog, walk him onto the training board, and give the command "Sit." Because he has been through the refinements I discussed in Chapter 7, he should obey and stay on the board. You should be able to walk around him and away from him without his moving. In preparation for throwing a retrieving dummy, position yourself between the dog and the spot where the dummy will fall. To envision this, think of a baseball diamond with the dog at home plate and you at the pitcher's mound. The dummy will be tossed over your shoulder to second base. If the dog breaks, you are in position to stop him before he gets to the dummy, and that's important. Remember, you have the check cord to help you grab him.

Once you've thrown the dummy over your shoulder— and if your dog has remained sitting—call his name for the retrieve. But if he comes off the board when you throw the dummy, pick him up, put him back on it, and push his rear down. Once he is sitting, send him for the retrieve by calling his name. In other words, your dog always gets the retrieve after he obeys and never gets it when he doesn't.

If your pup breaks and gets the dummy, take it out of his mouth without any fuss, toss it back where you first threw it, and return the dog to the board at home plate, making him sit without giving the verbal command. Once he has complied, allow him to make the second retrieve by calling his name. Remember that if you need to correct him, do so only at the board, because that's where he made the mistake (moving off it). If he breaks, gets to the dummy, and grabs it, do *not* scold him at second base, because he may interpret this as meaning that you do not want him to pick it up. As we've both said before, the correction must take place only at the point of disobedience.

In the process of line steadying, you should vary the length of time between the moment the dummy is thrown and the moment you call the dog's name. If you always wait exactly three seconds before releasing your pup for the retrieve, he will soon learn to wait for precisely that interval, then leave on his own. Remember: dogs are truly creatures of habit, and if you inadvertently create a bad one, it will be hard to undo.

Following success with the thrown-dummy drill, go to a clip-wing pigeon, repeating the drill exactly as it was done with the dummy. The dog should respond like a champ before you move on to the next stage.

Up to now, you yourself have been throwing the object to be retrieved. Now it is time for the dog to focus downfield, where all his birds will ultimately appear. One inexpensive way to develop line steadiness with downfield retrieves is to enlist the aid of one or more assistants. Stack two hay bales in two or three places in an open field. (A meadow that features a few scattered bushes or patches of brush will work, too.) Each assistant hides behind a bale stack and throws a bird. If you continually switch the stations from which the bird is thrown, the dog will never be sure where it is coming from.

The advantage of this approach is that the cost is limited to the dollars spent for a few pigeons and a six-pack for your buddies. The disadvantages are that assistants are not always available and that the dog will eventually key on hay bales as marking aids, or crutches. I prefer the use of remote launchers but recognize that not everyone is going to shell out several hundred dollars for a launching device and transmitter. However, I would be remiss if I did not describe your training options, leaving the economic decision up to you.

If you have decided to purchase a launcher, load it with a clip-wing pigeon and position the device downwind from your dog, so that he cannot smell the bird (in other words, the wind is blowing the bird scent away from the dog). Sit your pup on the board, put a check cord on him in case he breaks, then trigger the device and fire a shot. If the dog moves, pick him up, put him back on the board, and push his rear down—but do *not* give him the command "Sit." When he complies, send him for the retrieve. Again, vary the time between the fall of the clipwing and the moment when you call the dog's name.

At this stage, your pup's marking will be unaffected by the wait to retrieve because you are not asking him to make long pickups. Later in training, when you use flushed birds, don't make your dog wait too long, or he will get into the habit of turning around and looking at you before going to the mark. This will foster mismarking and encourage him to hunt for the bird instead of going straight to it and making a clean retrieve.

As for distances, start out by setting up the launcher and its clipwing about thirty-five yards from your dog. Then make the drill increasingly difficult by moving the launcher closer *in small increments*, so that you end up being able to launch birds just ten feet from your pup, while he remains steady on the board. As always, in demanding excellence, correct the dog when he fails, reward him when he succeeds. And remember, the biggest reward a talented flusher can get is the opportunity to retrieve a bird.

Once your pup remains sitting on the board reliably without your having to reinforce the "Sit" command after a bird is launched, he is ready to move on. As you recall, the board does nothing more than make it easier for your dog to understand that he is to remain sitting in one spot. Because canines are place-oriented, the board makes your job less painful and tedious. Less discipline is needed, and less discipline produces a more stylish and confident dog. But, at some point, you'll have to leave the board behind and re-

When your dog graduates from the board, treat drills as if the board were still in place.

peat the line-steadiness drills from the beginning. Treat your dog as if he were on an imaginary board. Anytime he breaks, do *not* repeat the "Sit" command—pick him up, put him back at the point of disobedience (the imaginary board), and make him sit with hand pressure. When he is reliable off the board, you can congratulate yourself, for you have a line-steady dog.

A line-steady dog should remain sitting regardless of the temptation.

Preparation for Steadiness to Flush

You can now begin teaching your dog that he must sit whenever a bird is in the air. The training board is not used in this exercise. Attach a twenty-foot check cord to the dog. While the dog is moving freely around you, tease him with a dummy or a clip-wing, or a lock-wing pigeon, building his excitement and desire for the retrieve. Then, when your pup is out in front of you and watching, throw the bird or dummy over your shoulder. The very moment it is in the air, give the dog the command "Sit."

Your dog must learn to sit when a bird is in the air.

At this point in the program, he *should* obey, but if he doesn't, you can stop him from getting to the dummy or bird because you are positioned between the mark and the dog, and you have a strong grip on the check cord. In case of an infraction, pick up the dog and put him back where he was when you issued the command (the imaginary board), and push his rear down. When the dog is sitting, send him for the retrieve. Always let your pup have the retrieve after he is sitting, even if he broke on the original attempt.

As always, short drills are preferable to long ones. A five- to ten-minute session is adequate. An ideal schedule would be three or four of these brief lessons each day. Don't drill the dog for hours on Saturday to make up the work you were unable to do Monday through Friday. Short, quality sessions are the key.

Once your pup is sitting down reliably at a voice command when the dummy or bird is thrown, you can move to a somewhat more complicated exercise, where the dog is beyond your immediate control. Go back to your groomed field, and plant a clip-wing or lock-wing pigeon at the ends of each row, as you did in pattern training. (As was the case in advanced patterning, don't let the dog see you make the plants.) If you don't have access to groomed rows, use the same training field that you relied on for pattern training.

At this point, don't use flyers because you no longer want him to chase. The reason for putting the non-flying birds in the field is to give your dog a reason to be there. (You simply want your pup to find and retrieve them.) As he quarters the field, he will quickly discover that there is something for him to pursue, so he will not watch you and wait for you to throw birds. In fact, you want to get beyond over-the-shoulder-bird drills as quickly as possible to avoid creating a dog that is focused on you. His job is to seek game in front of you.

Cast your dog as you did in the patterning drills. When he is coming down the rows from left to right but is still to the left of you, throw a clipwing to your right. That way you can get between your dog and the bird if he breaks. When you throw the bird up into the air, give the "Sit" command. If your dog breaks, prevent him from getting to the bird, then take him back to the spot where he disobeyed the command and silently push his butt down. Once he is sitting, send him for the retrieve. Again, vary the length of time that you make him sit before giving him the retrieve—anywhere from three to thirty seconds is plenty. Don't overdo it by making him sit too long. He may lose interest.

You might think that a check cord would be helpful in the drill I just described, but I don't like to run flushing dogs when they are dragging check cords. I want an excited, free-moving dog with a driving flush, not one that acts restrained or becomes conditioned to hunting that way. At this point in the program, the dog is certainly under enough control that I can get to him and return him to the point of disobedience.

If your pup breaks and somehow gets to the bird, don't run over and grab it from him, shake him, and scream in his face that he is a no good egg-sucker. He may think that you do not want him to touch birds. Keep quiet, calmly take the pigeon, and put it back where it fell. Then return your dog to the spot where he broke when you issued the command, and make him sit not with a verbal command but by firmly pushing his rear to the ground. Walk back to where you were when you originally issued the command, then call his name for the retrieve. If you have laid a proper foundation with the "Sit" .command prior to starting steadiness, this will go smoothly.

As in the steady-to-shot drills, the dog will associate the "Sit" command with the bird in the air if the exercise is repeated often enough. When it is obvious that your dog understands this lesson—that seeing the bird in the air is his command to sit—you should drop the verbal reinforcement.

At this point, your flusher should no longer need the

whistle or verbal command because individual elements in his learning chain are coming together. Earlier, you issued the command to "Sit" every time a bird was thrown, and he obeyed. Through repetition, he has learned that when a bird is in the air, the whistle or voice command to "Sit" is going to come. He has begun to sit automatically at the sight of the thrown clipwing. Once your dog is responding by sitting down on a thrown bird 100 percent of the time, you can move on to the next portion of steadiness training.

Finishing Steadiness to Flush and Shot

Here, you're going to use a combination of flyers and clipwings, and you will need a good many for this portion of steadiness training. Pigeons are the bird of choice because they are cheap and readily available. However, a dog that is steady on pigeons will not necessarily be steady on other birds. If you intend to hunt your dog on pheasants—or any larger species with a raucous flush—you will have to phase ringnecks into your training program at some point. But using pigeons first establishes the basis of steadiness and is kinder to your bank account.

To get started, attach a twenty-foot check cord to your dog's collar. Tell him "Sit," then walk about fifteen feet from him and toss a clipwing in front of you. If the previous steps in steadiness training have been completed correctly, the dog will remain sitting. If he does break, use the check cord to prevent him from grabbing the pigeon. Pick him up, take him back to where he broke, and make him sit, again by pushing his rear to the ground, not by issuing a verbal command.

Then call your dog's name and allow him to retrieve

this bird. It is important that approximately half the pigeons in this exercise be pickups. You do not want your pup to anticipate that every bird is going to fly; if he does, he may sit down prematurely. You are trying to develop a dog with an aggressive flush, not a dog that hangs up, points, or sits down when he sees a bird on the ground. If you intersperse clipwings with flyers, your pup will think that there's a chance he can catch every one. In other words, pickups will make your dog eager to pursue birds and will continue to build his confidence.

I need to emphasize what I said in the beginning of this chapter: The act of steadiness is unnatural to a spaniel or retriever. There is nothing in his genetic soup that makes your dog want to sit down at the flush of a bird. You must keep his confidence level high so that no bird-related problems are created during the steadiness procedure.

After you have conducted this drill a few times—that is, throwing a clipwing in front of you and allowing him to

Over time, you should increase the difficulty of steadying drills, eventually expecting your spaniel or retriever to be steady to flushed pigeons.

pick it up—switch to a flyer. This exercise will be much easier if you have a helper to serve as your gunner. (It's difficult to handle your dog on the check cord and simultaneously shoot the bird.) This helper should stand about ten yards to your left or right.

Again with the dog sitting about fifteen feet away from you and wearing a check cord, dizzy a flyer (*not* a clipwing) and throw it down. When the bird is up and walking around, call your dog's name. He will race to the pigeon, thinking that he is going to catch it as he has every other time. However, this bird will flush and get away from him. At the moment the flyer is up and cleanly away from the dog, give the "Sit" command by whistle or voice. If your pup does not obey at the flush or the command and chases the bird, stop him with the check cord. This will prevent him from getting the pigeon that your helper shoots.

Use a check cord to stop your pup if he fails to sit at a bird's flush.

It makes no difference whether the gunner hits or misses the bird. There will be misses in hunting situations, and your dog must remain steady to a missed bird as well as a shot bird. Often a flusher that is steady on a shot bird will break on a miss. So, it is important that in the steadying process your dog see birds that fly off untouched.

If your helper shoots a flyer and your pup has remained steady while marking the fall, call his name for the retrieve. On the other hand, if the gunner shoots the bird but your dog breaks, you should prevent him from getting the bird via the check cord. Pick him up, put him back on the spot where he broke,and firmly command him to "Sit." (Later in the program, you will want your dog to sit at a shot, a volunteer bird, or a flushed bird—without a verbal or whistle command. At this point, however, the reinforcement is needed.) If you feel that he has marked the fall, send him for the retrieve. If he did not mark the fall, don't worry about it. Simply have an assistant pick up the bird, or fetch it yourself. In the latter case, tell the dog to sit and leave him while you walk out to get the dead pigeon. (If he breaks, you already know precisely how to correct him.) There will be plenty of opportunities for him to discover that if he sits at the flush, he will get his reward—retrieving the bird.

Continue with this drill, randomly mixing pickups and flyers so that the dog won't predict that the next bird will be a flyer and respond by sitting down prematurely. If at any time you see that your pup is hesitating to drive in hard for the flush, go back to giving him pickups so that he starts boiling into the birds with confidence. Once again, short sessions are preferable to long ones.

Don't linger in this flushing exercise for an overly long period. You are simply trying to lock into the dog's mind that he is to sit down when he has moved a bird. You want your pup hunting aggressively in front of you—using his nose not his eyes—so do not run this drill more than necessary. The schedule will depend on the individual dog, but if you have followed instructions, a week of this exercise is usually enough. That means your pup will have played this game during two or three sessions of five to ten minutes each day for seven days.

At this point, the dog should be line steady, he should sit down when a clipwing is thrown in the field where he is running, and he should sit on the flush (with the check cord). Next, make the exercise a bit more demanding by conducting it with a mixture of pickups and flyers, but with no check cord. When your dog is consistently successful at this exercise, you are ready to move to the next level.

Here, too, you will need the assistance of a gunner. First, plant a few pickups in the field as you did in all your previous patterning drills. (The number of birds isn't critical. Simply alternate rows if you are using a groomed field.) Then, tuck a flyer and a couple of clipwings into your vest (you will see the reason for the clipwings in a moment). While your pup is running ahead—and not looking at you—dizzy and toss the flyer to the ground in front of you. It is important that the dog not catch you planting this bird, because you do not want him to get the idea that he should periodically stop running and look at you, waiting for you to throw a bird. You want him to keep hunting aggressively in front of you.

After you have tossed the flyer and walked past it, use the whistle to turn your dog back into the area of the plant, where he will smell the bird and drive in for the flush. When the bird goes airborne, immediately issue the command "Sit." If your pup remains steady to the flush, then your helper should shoot the bird. But if the dog breaks and chases, your helper should *not* kill the pigeon, because the retrieve would, in effect, reward the dog for disobeying. Go out and get your pup, put him back on the spot of the break, and give the "Sit" command again. Now throw one of the clipwings you squirreled away in your vest, so your dog understands that he gets a retrieve only if he sits and stays put.

If, during this exercise, a flyer is shot and your flusher breaks and beats you to the fall, go out and calmly take the bird as he comes in with it. Return the pigeon to the area of the fall, take your dog back to where he broke at the shot, and order him to sit (be stern when you do it). Then, walk to where you were standing when he broke, and send him for the retrieve. Again, it is not important that every bird be hit. Your flusher must learn to deal with misses, too.

As the dog flushes the planted flyers, continue using a verbal or whistle command to remind him to place his rear end solidly on the ground. Later, as he becomes reliable and learns that a flushed bird *always* means "Sit," drop the voice/whistle reinforcement.

Continue this drill until you can count on your dog's performing reliably. How will you know if your confidence level is high enough? Just remember the gamble mentioned in our discussion of retrieving corridors: Would you bet your last $10 that when your pup flushes a bird he will be steady to flush and shot? If not, the dog isn't ready to move to the next step.

And that is equally true in each of the building blocks that lead to steadiness. Your dog must be performing each task with excellence before you move on. Remember, every link in your dog's learning chain must be strong and well secured to the one before and the one that follows. Sooner than later, a weak link will show up, in which case the whole chain may fall apart. As we've said before, you can avoid such failures by using patience, persistence, and repetition.

Now that your dog is sitting on thrown birds, plant a 50/50 mixture of pickups and flyers in your training field.

A mix of flyers and clipwings creates a bold flush.

When your dog has flushed a flyer and the bird is in the clear, your assistant should shoot it. You, the handler, should wait for a few seconds, then walk up and pet your pup. Don't gush over him, just give him one quick "Good boy," then send him for the retrieve. You are instilling confidence in him by letting him know that he has done a good job of remaining steady.

If your helper misses the bird, cast your dog in a direction opposite that of the pigeon's flight (you don't want him to think that he is supposed to pursue that bird), then continue hunting down the field. Once again, don't call your dog to you when he is sitting after a flush; if you do, he will eventually get into the habit of coming back to you after he moves a bird.

If you have correctly followed the steps in this section on steadiness, the flush of a bird and the sound of a shot are now firmly associated with the "Sit" command. Indeed, they have *become* that command. Still, if at any time your pup breaks, catch him, pick him up, and put him back on the point of disobedience. The objective here is to end up with a dog that is steady without your shouting or whistling at him to sit, a gun dog that is under control and doing his job with a minimum of noise. And a spaniel or retriever in control—and one that hunts and finds birds with style—is a dog that you can be proud to show anyone, anywhere.

A dog that you trained to be steady to flush and shot is a dog that you can take pride in owning.

At this point in the program, although your pup is not yet finished, he now runs a polished pattern, hunts within gun range, and is steady to flush and shot. You can now hunt him on any upland game birds with the assurance that he is better trained than 95 percent of the other flushers you will see.

9.

Retrieving

There are two fundamental requirements if a dog is to become a fine retriever: exceptional marking ability and an excellent nose. Although there is no substitute for genetics, both of these traits can be honed by experience. The more opportunity your flusher has to mark and retrieve fallen birds, the better he will be at performing these duties.

A stylish retriever is developed over time through a combination of genetics, training, and experience.

However, most of us would prefer not to wait until a dog has five or six hunting seasons under his collar. Fortunately, appropriate training will accelerate his development into an outstanding retriever. You started this process early. Your pup had considerable experience with birds during your sessions in the retrieving corridor, and he got even more while picking up lockwings, clipwings, and shot flyers during patterning drills. Indeed, by this point in your dog's training, simply shooting numerous flyers for him will have improved his skills significantly. He should now be marking birds well and delivering them to you consistently.

However, before going any farther in this chapter—or in your training—please turn to and read carefully Appendix C, "The Conditioned Retrieve." This section deals with the process you may know better as "force-fetching," though some now consider that term to be politically incorrect. Whatever you call it, this process is critical if you want your dog to be a *superb* retriever, one that *always* delivers the bird to hand and with a firm yet gentle mouth. If, on the other hand, you are content with a flusher that retrieves with reasonable reliability and, say, drops the bird at your feet every time, you may choose not to put your dog on the training table.

That said, you should understand the force-fetching process and then make a *conscious* decision not to undertake it.

Marked Retrieves

Your dog's ability to mark—to pinpoint the location of the fall—can be improved if you do marking drills. Initially, you should conduct these exercises in a low-cut field, rather than in an area of high cover where your pup can't readily find thrown birds and training dummies. Ideally, you will have two helpers to do the throwing, and there is an important reason for this. If you always throw all the marks yourself, your pup will think that he should always look for the bird or dummy to emanate from your side. In real hunting situations, however, the bird (the eventual retrieve) will first appear well *ahead* of the gunner. Thus, the dog must learn to focus out in front and not fixate on the handler.

In addition, there is a limit as to how far you can hand-throw a dummy or bird, and your pup will get in the habit of running that distance and no more. Such retrieves are well short of the falls he will encounter in the field. By varying the positions of your helpers when they make their throws, you will help the dog learn to mark long falls as well as short ones.

To set up a marking drill, once again think of a baseball diamond, and picture yourself standing on the pitcher's mound. Start by placing one helper in left field and another in right field, both about thirty yards away. With your dog at your side, have one of the helpers call the dog's name (or whistle to get his attention), then toss a dummy. (It should be thrown in a high arc to make sure the dog sees it clearly, and it should not land too close to the assistant.) Send your dog for the retrieve. When he brings the dummy back and is repositioned at your side, have your other helper throw his dummy. Send the dog for that retrieve. As he runs out, backpedal toward home plate, and receive the bumper there. By gradually increasing the distance between you and your assistants, the dog will learn to sharpen his concentration on the mark.

Instead of dummies, you can use clip-wing pigeons in marking drills. These birds will fly twenty to thirty yards, forcing the dog to focus on the mark for a longer time.

Moreover, as always, live birds will instill more enthusiasm in your dog during these training exercises. So will using a gun shot to prompt your flusher to look for a mark. (Of course, it is imperative that your dog has been properly introduced to gunfire, as Joe Arnette discussed in Chapter 5, page 99.) With your flusher at your side, fire the gun, whether it is a .22 blank pistol or a shotgun with popper loads. At the shot, your assistant should throw the mark. When it hits the ground, send your dog.

He should be line-steady or steady to wing and shot at this point. However, there is no such thing as a perfect dog. If he does break or creep forward in marking drills, return him to the original spot where you first commanded "Sit," and firmly push his rear to the ground. Do *not* repeat the verbal command. Some handlers use a riding crop, quirt, or heeling stick at this point, to reinforce steadiness. I prefer the electronic collar for correction. However, *this is not an option unless the dog has been thoroughly collar conditioned,* as outlined in Appendix B, "Introduction to Training with Electronics." When the dog breaks, I administer the previously determined minimal level of stimulation and leave it on until I have returned the dog to the place of the infraction.

If you do not have assistants to help you with marking drills, electronic bird launchers, though expensive, are a marvelous training tool. You can position them at various distances in the field, just as you would helpers. Once you're back with the dog, fire the gun, trigger one of the launchers, and send your dog for the retrieve. As long as your flusher was born and bred with excellent marking ability, the more drills you do, the more his skills will improve. Initially, however, limit each session to two marks. As the dog progresses, you can give him more. For the average flusher, I think a half-dozen marks per session is more than enough in the advanced stages of training. The key is

An electronic bird launcher is a marvelous training tool for retrieving and marking drills.

to keep these exercises fun, thereby creating a stylish and enthusiastic retriever.

You can also use a handheld launcher to hone your pup's retrieving abilities. As described earlier, this device fires a canvas or PVC dummy by way of a powerload charge (essentially a .22 blank). Depending on the load, you can achieve distances of up to two hundred feet, which are impossible if you're throwing the dummy by hand. Again, however, the primary disadvantage of the handheld launcher is that the mark originates at your side, whereas in actual hunting situations, the bird will be shot out in front of your dog.

Electronic launchers, on the other hand, allow you to more closely duplicate reality. There are no assistants for your dog to key on, so he will have to learn to mark more efficiently. Also, the action does not originate at your side; it is always out in front of your pup. You fire the gun and then launch the bird. At the shot, the dog looks for a mark, sees it, and concentrates on the area of the fall.

Remember, dogs are creatures of habit. If you always give your dog forty-yard retrieves, he will more often than not come up short on sixty-yard marks. By varying the distance of the falls, you will give your dog valuable marking experiences and teach him not to expect a specific distance for his retrieving work.

Before you move on to the next stage in training—blind retrieves—your flusher should be absolutely proficient at marking falls in a variety of cover and at distances from ten to a hundred yards. Moreover, he must consistently sit *immediately* on a single voice or whistle command. Once you are sure of him in both respects, you can begin work on blinds. However, this will be a stressful transition for your pup, and you may want to mix in some straightforward marking drills now and then to maintain the dog's enthusiasm and confidence.

Blind Retrieves

If, for whatever reason, a flusher in the field is unable to mark a particular fall, most upland hunters will walk the dog into the area of the fall and tell him to find the bird. But sometimes, this isn't possible. Imagine that you are hunting pheasants along a cattail marsh, and while the dog is in the thick cover, you shoot a bird that falls well out into water. Odds are that you won't want to wade through muck and hip-deep water to get your dog to the area of the fall. He must learn to do this on his own, under your guidance.

Blind retrieves are based on trust. If the dog thinks he knows better than you where the fall is, he will search where he wants, not where you want. Let's say a hunting partner on your right shoots a pheasant thirty yards ahead of where he's walking. Your flusher is on the left and hears the shot, but he does not see the bird fall twenty yards to your right, well out in front of your partner. The dog will naturally want to hunt in the direction from which the shot came. However, he must believe that he will find the bird only by taking your directions on a blind retrieve. This trust must be taught and this training will take a lot of effort.

In teaching blind retrieves, owners often demand too much too soon. Training a dog to perform blind retrieves competently requires many steps, each one of which must be mastered before a dog can achieve such high-level performance.

The preparation for blind retrieves takes place on land. Your dog *must* be proficient at blind retrieves on dry ground before progressing to water work. The training situation is much more controllable on land, and it is folly to expect a dog to succeed in water if he fails in, say, a mowed field. For example, if he picks up a dummy on land and scoots in the opposite direction, you can expect the same rebellious antics from him in the water. He will not be the first retriever to take the dummy to the opposite bank and challenge you with, "What are you going to do about it?" Do not set yourself up for this kind of failure. Stay on land as long as necessary.

If you're able to set up a retrieving alley in your training field, by all means do so. It will be a tremendous benefit to you and your dog as he learns the business of blind retrieves. If you have access to a field that you can mow, use a bush hog or lawn tractor to cut a long strip—up to a hundred yards in length—down the field, leaving "walls" of high grass on either side. You can then position an electronic bird launcher or hidden assistant at the end of this lane. When your dog sees a bird or bumper go skyward, he can and will run straight down the alley and quickly find the mark. Such success creates the confidence that he can always come up with the bird, even when the alley isn't there to show him the way.

The hundred-yard mowed retrieving corridor will build your pup's trust and teach him to run hard, straight lines. Walk him out about twenty yards, and throw a dummy down. Walk the dog back to the beginning of the alley, sit him down, and—if the dog is on your left—flatten your left hand as if you were going to deliver a karate chop and position it slowly along the right side of the dog's face, pointing it toward the mark. (If you heel and sit him on your right, put your right hand along the left side of his face.)

The proper hand and arm position when lining up a dog for a blind retrieve.

Send your pup on the command "Back," which he will come to recognize as a cue that he is to make a blind retrieve. Gradually vary the length of the retrieves in the corridor, which are often referred to as "sight blinds." This is a memory game, and it teaches your dog that when you send him, there is always a bird for him to pick up. Occasionally—with the dog watching—place a dummy at about twenty yards, another one at twenty-five yards, and a third one at thirty yards. Send your pup for each one in succession to reinforce his running a straight line. As he masters this "lining drill," extend the distance between the dummies in the series.

Once your dog is performing well in these exercises, leave him in his crate and place a dummy in the mowed path without his seeing the plant. Bring the dog to the beginning of the alley, walk him to within ten yards of the dummy, line him toward the mark with your hand, and then give him the command "Back." Because there has always been something in the cut path for him to retrieve in the past, he will expect something again and should run to get it. (If he balks, or refuses to go, return to the sight blinds already discussed.) As before, gradually increase the length of these simple blind retrieves, moving out five yards at a time. Once the dog can be sent the entire length of the alley (about a hundred yards), you are ready to move to left and right blind retrieves, using the command "Over."

Your training field should now be mowed to create two paths that intersect at right angles, forming a cross. Think of it as a baseball diamond, where the pitcher's mound is at the center; from there, the paths lead to home plate and to first, second, and third base, respectively. Walk your pup at heel from the intersection of the two paths (the mound) to second base, and toss down a dummy. Then return him to the mound and command "Sit." You, the handler, should go to home plate and turn so that you and the dog are facing each other.

Use the command "Back"—accompanied by an exaggerated hand motion—to send your pup for the dummy behind him. The signal involves raising your arm straight over your head, with your palm turned toward the dog to make your hand as visible as possible. Thrust your arm forward—toward second base—as you give the verbal command. Repeat this exercise until your pup is performing with excellence on "Back" and will move quickly from the pitcher's mound to second base even if you haven't shown him the dummy first.

Your dog can be taught right and left blind retrieves in the same fashion. Start by placing a bumper or dead bird toward first base while the dog is watching, then return to home plate. To release the dog, give the command "Over," while extending your arm straight out toward first base, keeping it parallel to the ground. Once the dog has become accomplished at right blind retrieves of various lengths, teach him left blind retrieves using the same method but the other arm. Now you can put piles of dummies at all three bases and gradually begin to alternate "Over" (left hand) with "Back" and "Over" (right hand) until your pup is consistently taking all your casts correctly and picking up the right dummies.

When the dog is reliable on the mowed rows of your "baseball diamond," it is time to move your work on blind retrieves and handling to an ungroomed field. Start off in fields with no more than foot-high grass, and begin with a simple drill involving just "Back." With the dog in the crate where he cannot see you, place a dummy or lock-wing pigeon ten yards from an imaginary pitcher's mound, making sure that the wind is blowing from the dummy or bird to the spot from which you are going to send the dog. You will now repeat each step you followed in teaching blind retrieves on the mowed baseball diamond. When the dog is solid on a particular cast, move to the next one. But, if his performance is shaky on any one cast, building on it will lead to eventual failure, resulting in confusion or outright disobedience.

Confusion should be dealt with by restoring your pup's confidence with drills he has already mastered and is comfortable with. Go back to a cast he always takes, shorten up distances, or even return to the mowed paths. On the other hand, disobedience—if that is, in fact, the correct diagnosis—must be dealt with immediately and firmly. Returning the dog to "boot camp" (yard drills designed to reinforce his obedience of basic commands like "Sit") will often restore an enthusiastic "Yes, sir!" attitude.

A top retriever in action is a joy to watch.

Teaching blind retrieves takes hours, days, and weeks of diligent training. Do *not* try to rush the process. This is complicated learning for your dog, and in this case, patience is a virtue. But the effort is certainly worthwhile. A flusher that is capable of performing blind retrieves is a joy to watch, conserves game, and is a dog of which an owner can be truly proud.

10.

Training Your Flusher to Cope with Running Birds

Tracking is a learned skill. Nature endows well-bred dogs with an olfactory arsenal, but they have to learn how to use it. Some individual gun dogs seem born to be fine trackers, and certain breeds exhibit higher-caliber tracking skills than others. Nonetheless, given experience, all dogs can learn to become proficient at following birds that are moving on the ground.

In most of your training to date, you used pigeons—either dizzied flyers, clipwings, or lockwings. In any case, the bird always remained close to the spot where you planted it (and if the dizzied pigeon flew away, there was no track for your dog to take). In other words, until now, there was always a bird where your dog thought it was or, at worst, a short trail when the plant wandered a bit.

This kind of drill is fine for preparing your pup for game like woodcock, which hold tight. But if you are developing a pheasant dog, you need to remember that these birds are runners as much as flyers. They have a tendency to move on the ground—and move fast—to escape any threat. Ruffed grouse will run, too, though to a lesser extent. Thus, your dog must learn to track moving game instead of deciding that just because a bird didn't flush, it is no longer around. You don't want your pup to give up on one bird to search for another that stays put. He must learn to put his nose to the ground and unravel the maze of departing foot scent. A flushing dog that does not learn tracking skills will be inept on moving birds and will not get top honors as an upland hunter, let alone as a pheasant or grouse specialist.

There is no substitute for practice when a dog is learning to track running birds. Of course, your pup can gain this experience over time during his hunting career, but there is no legitimate reason not to train your pup to track moving birds relatively early in his life.

The Fundamentals of Tracking

You can jump-start a youngster by using released quail. After your dog has been introduced to birds—when he is twelve to fourteen weeks old—hold him by the collar (or stake him out), free some quail, and let him watch as they walk away into light cover. Don't reprimand your pup if he lunges for the quail. Just keep quiet and restrain him until the birds have disappeared. Then release him. He will run to the area where he last saw the quail and probably put his nose down and start trying to track them.

Later, when you begin formally honing the tracking skills of your dog, take him out on a dark, overcast night to handicap his sight. For this exercise, you should use a live duck with a strip of tape or Velcro wrapped around its primary wing feathers to preclude flight. Make your dog sit, then toss the duck down in front of him, in plain view. Now, however, shine a flashlight in your dog's face to prevent him from watching the bird waddle away into cover. Give the duck a few minutes' head start, then release your dog. He will run to the spot where he saw the duck land, but instead of finding a bird, he will discover grass full of strong scent. The duck will have dragged his oily rear end through the cover, leaving a scent trail that most dogs could follow with cotton in their nostrils. After a few of these drills (the number will vary with individual pups), your dog will understand that he can use his nose to track a bird that has hotfooted it away from a resting point.

These exercises are important, because your novice tracker *must* come to understand that he should always check an area for the telltale foot scent that indicates a bird is running. This concept is best taught—initially, at least—under controlled conditions. The problem with letting your dog gain his tracking degree solely on wild birds is that most of the pheasants and grouse that use running as an escape tactic are veterans, individuals that have successfully avoided predators for some time. They are professionals at dodging and zigzagging. These survivors will most often elude a young dog, and if he is consistently unable to produce birds, he may quit and not put forth an honest effort to find running game. Your pup needs to succeed from the outset in order to develop the confidence required of a consistently fine tracker. So, the tape- or Velcro-restrained duck is an excellent choice for introductory tracking exercises because the bird leaves such a heavy scent trail.

I do not advocate the practice of tying a scented dummy or a bird—whether dead or alive—to a string and pole, and dragging it through the cover. Use these alternative methods if you must, but be aware that human foot scent will accompany all of these scent trails. This might not be a problem if your dog hunts wild birds exclusively, but it may produce an undesirable result at hunting preserves and at field trials. Here, the bird planters must walk the cover to put out game. As I discussed in Chapter 6, dogs will take the path of least resistance by following the human foot scent straight to birds. After enough drills where human scent leads to a bird, your dog will make the connection. Hence, you may actually produce a dog that hunts for human foot scent, rather than feathers.

That's why I prefer to use live birds in my drills. Eventually, I want to train with the species that I expect my dogs to hunt. (This is not always possible, however, as exemplified by ruffed grouse; pen-raised birds are not available.) If I am developing a pheasant dog, I ultimately expose him to pheasants as a training bird. Initially, I secure the wings with tape or Velcro and shackle the legs to make it easier for the youngster to succeed. Even a pen-raised pheasant is trickier and more elusive than a duck. (To shackle a pheasant, tie a four-inch piece of rope between the bird's feet, securing each end with a slip knot. This will prevent the pheasant from stretching its legs and disappearing into the sunset.) Remember, in order to build the dog's confidence, it is important that he succeed in the primary stages of tracking.

By the way, guinea fowl are also excellent birds for tracking drills. They are heartier than pheasants and wear the same track shoes. An added plus is that they will return voluntarily to a recall pen, which allows you to use the same birds repeatedly.

After your dog gets the hang of tracking hobbled pheasants and/or guinea fowl, move to unshackled birds. Sure, these larger species are expensive and some will escape your pup, but producing a dog that can trail and flush a wild-running pheasant or ruffed grouse is well worth losing a few dollars.

As is so often true with training drills, there can be a negative side to conducting too many tracking exercises. By overdoing them, you may encourage your flusher to run with his head down, checking for ground scent instead of taking air scent with his head high. This, in turn, may produce a dog that pushes birds downfield, instead of putting them into the air. So, stay with these drills long enough for your pup to grasp the idea of tracking birds—but no longer.

Stopping on Runners

Teaching your dog to stop when he is tracking running birds is a strategy that will put more game in the bag while maintaining a high level of safety. A hunter who is carrying a loaded gun and trying to keep up with a dog that is chasing a running bird is an accident waiting to happen. Moreover, this practice is not only unsafe but also ineffective.

Let's say you are out hunting pheasants with your flusher. He is quartering into the wind when, suddenly, he whirls and makes game. It is obvious that the rooster is running. Your dog unravels the escape path and takes off in full pursuit of the running bird. The dog and pheasant are moving more quickly than you can follow safely. When your flusher gets to the edge of comfortable gun range, you command him to sit—either verbally or with one whistle blast. Your dog responds by dropping his posterior to the ground. You move up at a safe speed, then release the dog by saying "Hie on" or "Okay" or whatever release command you chose during your early training sessions.

The dog resumes tracking. Every time he gets too far

out, you sit him down and move up. In this manner, the dog eventually flushes the pheasant within gun range and gives you a reasonable opportunity of dropping the bird. Understand that using this technique doesn't mean that your pup will produce every running bird, but those he does flush will be within gun range. Watching birds flush sixty yards downfield with a dog in full pursuit is very frustrating. Chasing the dog over rough terrain with a loaded gun is just plain dangerous.

The "how to" of teaching your pup to stop on running birds is not complicated. First he must reliably respond to the command "Sit" or "Hup" under *any* conditions. If you cannot sit your dog down at a distance of thirty yards in the absence of game, it is foolish to expect to stop him when he is hotly pursuing a moving bird. The first step toward achieving this higher level of performance is to reinforce the "Sit" command, which was discussed in Chapter 7.

It is not mandatory that your dog be steady to wing and shot in order to teach him to sit on command when pursuing a running bird. However, a dog trained to this level is a flusher already in control. Stopping on hotfooting game birds is certainly a tough test of control, and a dog sitting reliably at the flush and shot will more readily learn to stop on runners. This is precisely why I discussed steadying to wing and shot first, in an earlier chapter.

Once you have reassured youself that can stop your dog at any distance, you are ready to tempt him with birds. Go back to the training board and give the whistle command, "Sit." Then toss a lock-wing pigeon roughly ten yards from the dog. If he moves, pick him up, return him to the board, and push his rear end down—without a verbal command. Your dog should perform this exercise with excellence, every time. (Although it is not absolutely necessary, you

A dog trained to stop on a whistle command, in the face of game, is a dog in control.

may want to expand and reinforce this drill, on the board, using a shackled pheasant.) Finally, move your dog off the board and repeat the exercise with lockwings and then clip-wings, making corrections—when necessary—at the point of disobedience.

If the dog is chasing a clipwing, fails to sit on the whis-tle command, and catches the bird, simply take it from him. Toss the pigeon down where you met the dog and return him to the spot where you told him "Sit." Remember, do *not* repeat the whistle command. Push the dog's rear end to the ground emphatically and, after he complies and remains sitting, release him and let him catch and retrieve the bird. This way your flusher learns that he will only get his re-ward—the clipwing—if he sits at your command and re-mains sitting.

When your dog is consistently succeeding off the board with pigeons, use tape or a Velcro strap to secure a pheasant's wings so it cannot fly, and hobble the bird so it cannot run too far, too fast. (See the instructions presented earlier in this chapter.) For this drill, use a low-cut field so the dog can see the bird as it runs. Snap a check cord onto your pup's collar. Now give the "Sit" command with your whistle, and toss out the pheasant. The dog should remain stationary. He should have this drill down pat.

Once the pheasant runs, release your dog; he should take off after the escaping bird. As he moves away from you, give him the whistle command to sit. If he obeys, walk to him, praise him, and release him so that he can resume the chase. If he doesn't stop, do *not* give the command again. Instead, catch him by the check cord, and return him to the imaginary board. With enough repetitions, you will have a dog that you can stop on a running bird.

Here again, there is a risk to overdoing these exercises. If you constantly stop your dog after sending him for a retrieve or when he is tracking and chasing runners, he may develop a hesitant flush. A dog that is stopped constantly may anticipate the "Sit" command upon seeing or smelling game and may actually sit down before flushing or pursuing the bird. In order to avoid this undesirable trait, mix plenty of clipwings into your drills, and let the dog drive in and catch them. If your pup isn't stopped but is allowed to grab at least half of these birds, his flush will remain strong.

Teaching a dog to stop on runners is worth the investment you need to make in training time and live birds. You will end up with a dog in complete control which, in turn, will assure you greater success in the field.

Appendices

Appendix A:
Nutrition Basics

Your flushing dog is an athlete, and you must feed him like one. Considering all of the expenses associated with developing your dog into a fine gunning companion, attempting to save money by giving him an inferior food is an unwise decision. A proper diet is critical to his performance in the field.

Nutrition is a complex subject. However, today's top dog-food companies employ professional animal nutritionists to develop premium maintenance and performance foods that are better than ever. Premium foods provide your dog with quality, balanced ingredients that, when accompanied by a sound conditioning program, will ensure he stays fit, trim, and healthy. In order to perform his job with style and vitality, your dog must eat a balanced diet that will support his energy needs. With all the information and misinformation that bombards consumers concerning dog foods, making the right choice is not always easy.

Your dog gets energy from proteins, carbohydrates, and

fats. Protein is made up of a long string of amino acids. When your dog digests protein, his system breaks it up into individual amino acids, which are used to rebuild muscle, skin, and hair. If your dog digests more protein than his body needs as a source of amino acids, the additional protein will be converted to energy. However, because the body prefers to get its energy from fats and carbohydrates, protein is its last resort. But as a gun dog works hard, he depletes his fat and carbohydrate supplies, which means he must rely on protein for the extra energy he needs.

Thus, the main function of protein in the diet is not to supply energy, but to provide amino acids. Assuming your dog is generally healthy, an insufficiency of protein typically appears first as a loss of hair quality—the dog's body has more important things to do with its limited protein supply. A healthy, but relatively inactive dog needs a diet featuring about 18 percent protein. Thus, if he were given a food that included 20 percent protein, the additional 2 percent would be available as an energy source. This might be sufficient for an animal that isn't being hunted. However, when your dog is working hard on a regular basis, he requires more protein to rebuild muscle tissue. If his protein intake does not increase to meet those additional requirements, there will be no protein available as an energy source.

In the wild, canines (like coyotes and wolves) eat few carbohydrates; they get their energy primarily from proteins and fats. However, carbohydrates are an excellent source of energy, and today's premium dog foods contain a mix of proteins, carbohydrates, and fats. The benefits of this blend are not merely nutritional. Dog-food manufacturers use carbohydrates to bind the dry kernels of ingredients like bone meal into bite-size kibble. There is also an economic advantage to the consumer, because carbohydrate sources such as rice and flour are considerably cheaper than chicken meal and dehydrated chicken fat.

It takes a minimum of three hours before a dog begins to benefit from a feeding and at least eight to sixteen hours before he will completely digest his food. Therefore, feeding your dog in the morning, just before you turn him loose on a bird hunt is ill-advised. Not only will your dog receive little benefit from the feeding, but you also increase the possibility of bloat.

Bloat itself is not life-threatening. However, it may cause a condition called Gastric-Volvulus Dilation. There are two ways GVD can kill your dog. One is where the stomach and/or the intestines flip. Imagine a hot-dog shaped balloon that twists at the ends—that's what goes on inside the dog. The other way GVD can kill your dog is when the stomach twists into the shape of a bobby pin. If your dog ever looks and acts as if he swallowed a basketball, get to a vet quickly; you have twenty minutes *at most* before your hunting companion will die.

So, think twice about a pre-hunt "He-Man Breakfast." It is not wise to ask your dog's digestive system to fully break down the fats and proteins supplied by a full feeding while he exercises. An evening feeding supplemented with snacking is the right prescription. Snacking is good. Here is where carbohydrates are of value to hunters. If you are going to give a snack to your dog—and there is a benefit to doing so—give him carbohydrates. Carbohydrates are converted to energy much more quickly than either fats or proteins.

Therefore, if you feed your dog a handful of cooked rice flour or wheat flour mixed with a couple of tablespoons of corn syrup in the morning before a hunt, he will have an increased energy source to tap. The same snack is a good idea during your noontime lunch break in the field, for it will replenish your dog's supply of carbohydrates and glucose (blood sugar). Complex sugars, such as those found in corn syrup, provide a longer energy boost than simple sugars, like those in table sugar. Keep in mind, however, that ingesting sugar causes the body to produce insulin. Although your dog will receive an initial energy rush from the corn syrup, the accompanying insulin boost will ultimately act as a "downer."

The third source of energy in a dog's diet is fat. Fat is two-and-a-half times more effective as an energy source than protein or carbohydrates. Think of fat as a time-release pill. Fat is there for the long haul, enabling your dog to continuously draw on his "fat tank" over extended periods of high energy demand. None of the premium dog-food companies put much more than 20 percent fat in their kibble. But that level of fat content will supply less than 50 percent of the energy a hard-working gun dog needs. If you take time off each fall and hunt your dog steadily—more than just a Saturday here and there—boosting the fat intake of his diet can give him a real advantage.

Canola oil is an excellent source of additional fat. Mixing a couple of tablespoons into the dog's daily food will aid in maintaining his energy and drive during a busy hunting season. With increased exercise and a higher fat intake, your dog's metabolism will burn the contents of his fat tank before emptying his glucose tank. This means he will have more energy available over a longer period of time. And that's what you want in a dog that must perform over a long bird season. A diet that is appropriately high in fat enables gun dogs to draw on fat as the major supplier of energy, rather than diverting protein from its important muscle-building duties.

Several manufacturers produce special performance foods containing approximately 30 percent protein and 20 percent fat. With supplementation that should depend on activity levels, this combination will supply your dog with sufficient fat and protein to sustain the high energy demanded of a hard-working dog. Note that the 30/20 ratio is a useful guideline, for there is a definite relationship between the required percentage of fat and corresponding protein. Which brings us to the most important feature of your dog's diet—balance. The term "optimal nutrition" refers to a diet that provides the proper balance of energy to protein, calcium to phosphorus, insoluble fiber to soluble fiber, and essential fatty acids/vitamin E to polyunsaturated fats. As I said, nutrition is complex.

Let me make it simpler by offering a few rules of thumb to supplement those Joe Arnette presented in Chapter 3, page 34. Generally, it is advisable to buy a food that lists the manufacturer, not the distributor. This way you know precisely who guarantees the quality and content of the food. For an active, healthy, working gun dog, select a food with something like the aforementioned 30 percent protein/20 percent fat ratio. During the off season a diet of 26 percent protein and 15 percent fat will normally supply the less active dog with its energy needs. Chicken or chicken-byproduct meal is the preferred first-listed ingredient on the bag, primarily because it is more digestible than other types of meal like beef or lamb. Unfortunately, however, the fine print will not tell you about the quality of these ingredients. Good chicken or chicken-byproduct meal and fat costs more than poor meal or fat. Manufacturers of fine, premium foods use higher-grade ingredients and more exacting quality-control procedures, and these factors are reflected in the higher cost of their products.

But the rewards of keeping a first-class flushing dog in prime condition more than justify spending the extra money.

Appendix B: Introduction to Training With Electronics

Back in the figurative Dark Ages, when dogs and electricity were just getting to know one another, electronic collars were big, bulky gizmos attached to the animal with heavy-duty harness leather. Those primitive shock collars didn't have great range, but what they lacked in long-distance utility they more than made up for with close-in knockdown power. Their single level of intensity—high—packed enough juice to put a buffalo on its knees. They were punishment tools, pure and simple.

It was in the 1950s that electronic collars were first devised and used in the field. They had one function—to break dogs of unwanted behavior like chasing deer or to correct disobedience such as a dog's refusing to come when called. And *break*—not *train*—was the operative word with early electronics. When a dog transgressed, he discovered quickly that lightning could and would strike from a distance.

A case can be made that those who adopted the original remote electronics treated problems with harsh and unsophisticated medicine, lacked any behavioral knowledge of dogs, and made no attempt to differentiate between training and breaking. A good many gun dogs were, indeed, broken: they lost enthusiasm, became fearful of doing their work, or were permanently case-hardened.

On the flip side, a more compelling argument says that the mistakes made and knowledge gained during those early years allowed remote collars and their intelligent use to mature and bloom in the 1990s. The more visionary trainers recognized the potential in the humane use of electronics and, in concert with engineers, developed the remote technology that we have today. As hands-off *training* aids, E-collars have come far since the days when dogs wore humongous batteries around their necks and were fried for any error.

Modern electronic collars are no different than any other training device or method: If applied incorrectly they can produce negative, even disastrous, results. But when they are used appropriately, they are a marvelous tool. Always keep in mind that remote electronics are not magic devices that instantly transform all who own them into professional trainers and turn all dogs that wear them into blue-ribbon hunters.

If you decide to work with an electronic collar, you should purchase one that has both variable intensity levels and a continuous-stimulation mode that stays on as long as you depress the control button (up to the ten-second maximum). Before you even take it out of the box, however, you must understand that using the outdated concept of punishment training as your sole approach will typically result in a dog that responds to commands only when he is afraid of being disciplined. If you establish punishment as your training base, be assured that as soon as your pup is off the check cord and not wearing electronic jewelry, he will say to hell with you and do as he chooses. A gun dog trained strictly with punishment, is a dog that performs inconsistently and without motivation, if he performs at all.

Fundamentally, punishment training bypasses the critical first two stages of the four-stage conditioning program described in Chapter 4. It leaps straight into giving a command—even one that the dog may not understand—then punishes him for disobedience. Such a dog is given limited initial training and few, if any, incentives to obey a command before punishment is administered.

This approach is taken by too many novice users of electronic collars, and it is precisely where they go wrong. Let's say your dog is out of control—he ranges too wide and won't come when you call him. So you get an electronic collar to fix the problem. You strap it on, cast your dog, then command him to come. But he is out there running around and having a fine time, so he ignores you. In response, you put the juice to him. At that point, your dog will do one of three things: First, he may run away from you as far as he can, as fast as he can. After ten seconds, the transmitter's shocking stimulation will turn off automatically (a programmed-in safety feature). Second, again because he hasn't been taught what the stimulation means, your pup may "freeze" in place and endure the discomfort for the ten seconds it takes the stimulation to shut off. Third, the dog may run back to you cowering and completely confused.

In the first case, you have essentially taught your dog that if he bolts, the discomfort will stop. In the second instance, he learns that if he grits his teeth for a short period, he can make the pain disappear. Either way, you have just taken the first steps along the road to case-hardening him and necessitating the use of ever-increasing levels of punishment. In the third scenario, when your pup runs back to your side and the stimulation goes away, he may soon consider any place out in front of you to be dangerous and see his only option as clinging to your bootlaces. In all three cases, you may have taught him to turn off stimulation by doing exactly what you don't want him to do—run, freeze or potter.

Strapping on a collar and using stimulation immediately is absolutely the wrong way to introduce your gun dog to remote electronics. To maximize the many training benefits of this equipment, you must approach the process in a rational manner. The underlying value of the electronic collar is that when used properly, it will produce a dog that is bold and confident, a happy dog that performs with enthusiasm.

The first step in a sensible program for introducing your dog to remote electronics must be to accustom your pup to the physical presence and feel of an E-collar around his neck. For about two months prior to actually applying any stimulation, let him wear a collar each time you take him out for a run. You can use either a dummy collar, which is a non-functional replica of the actual thing, or a deactivated real collar that is turned off or has its batteries removed. In a short time, when your pup spots the collar in your hand, he will be enthusiastic and ready to go.

Very simply, he will have linked the sight and feel of the electronic unit with having fun. Hence, his association with the collar is positive and will remain so. Your pup will not view it as a punishment tool—as he might if you had strapped it on and shocked him the first time out. This reduces the risk that you will create a dog that obeys commands inappropriately and inconsistently out of fear. Moreover, putting the collar on the dog frequently and *not* using any stimulation (a practice that should continue throughout his life) will prevent his becoming "collar-wise" and responding only when he is wearing the device.

The proper time to introduce your pup to electronic stimulation—that is, to teach him how to turn it off—is when you are ready to move into formal training. By this, I mean when you are beginning to refine the dog's response to basic commands by using correction. This process is described in Chapter 7; the difference is that you will replace hands-on stimuli (like pushing down the dog's rear) with electronic stimuli.

Because this appendix is geared to *introducing* your pup to remote electronics, it focuses only on teaching the four yard commands—"Kennel," "Sit," "Here," and "Heel." To take a description of electronic training beyond that basic level requires a book in itself. My goal, here, is to provide you with the fundamentals of appropriate E-collar use. When you complete the program presented below, you can choose not to go farther, or you can move on to intermediate and advanced electronic training with the help of a professional and/or some of the books in our "Selected Bibliography." Whatever your choice, your dog will have had a solid introduction to electronics.

First, I would strongly suggest your reviewing the four learning stages that Joe Arnette first outlined in Chapter 4: Show Pup (including the four basic yard commands); Stimulus-Command-Response; Command-Stimulus-Response; and Command-Response. Remember, up to the point of introducing actual electronic stimuli to teach particular commands, you have been in the no-correction, "Show Pup" stage.

Only after your dog has learned to love the collar by wearing one (without any stimulation) for several months, and only when he knows the basic commands via many repetitions of "Show Pup," should you begin electronic training that involves correction. Note that during this stage, you will use only the collar's continuous-stimulation mode, *not* the momentary-stimulation mode that remains active for only a fraction of a second, regardless of how long you depress the button.

First, you must find the lowest intensity level to which your dog responds. Keep in mind that dogs are individuals, so the level that works for one may not be appropriate for another. Don't assume that because your pup has shown a tendency to be "hardheaded" that he will require the highest level. Nor is it a sure thing that your friend's "soft" dog will need the lowest level. Electronic training doesn't work that way.

If you have never before used an E-collar, try it on yourself before strapping one on your dog (if you are afraid to be your own guinea pig, ethically you shouldn't use this device on your dog). Hold the transmitter in one hand and the collar's receiving unit in the other so that both contact points (electrodes) firmly touch your forefinger or palm. Try as many intensities as you can handle. You may not even feel some of them, while higher levels will indeed shock you. Another factor to keep in mind is that your dog will be wearing the collar around his neck, a far more sensitive area than your hand.

The electronic collar should be placed high on your dog's neck and be cinched tight enough to ensure constant contact between the unit's electrodes and the underpart of the dog's neck. A loose collar may not provide the instantaneous, continuous stimulation that you will require. At best, the sensation your dog feels will be intermittent and unpredictable, and it won't teach him that he can turn off the pressure by obeying the command you have just issued.

To find the proper intensity for your pup, begin with the lowest level and keep the continuous stimulation button depressed. Look for signs of movement or slight changes in demeanor. Perhaps your dog was panting and when stimulation began, he stopped for a moment. He might turn his head and look at you as he feels this new sensation. You can also place your fingers on his neck, just beneath his ear, and feel for an involuntary muscle twitch when you apply stimulation. If you see or feel no response at one level, move up to the next until your dog shows movement or some other small physical reaction *without yelping or panicking*. This should be the stimulation level that you use to introduce your pup to electronics.

The beauty of this approach is that it allows your dog to show you the proper level of correction for him. Traditional, "non-electronic" training manuals commonly tell readers to "use the appropriate amount of correction." But what *is* the appropriate amount (say, with a crop), and how do you determine it? With the electronic collar, you know which level to use because you can see its subtle effects. In this way, electronic training is more direct and clearcut than traditional means, which makes it easier to learn.

Note that the following program describes using the E-collar exclusively, after "Show Pups" for training yard commands. That is the approach I favor. However, if you would feel more comfortable with a conservative approach, you can teach the commands using the traditional methods I presented in Chapter 7. Then, as your confidence increases, you can polish your dog's performance by taking him through the introductory E-collar program.

Once you have determined the minimum level of stimulation that affects your dog, you are ready to teach him how to turn it off. (Again, you are going to be reinforcing basic commands he already knows from your work with "Show Pups.") Snap a check cord on your dog's E-collar, and stand two to three feet in front of a Vari-Kennel type crate with its door removed or tied open. Allow enough slack in the check cord for your dog to move easily into the crate, but not so much that you lose the benefit of control. (You may have to use the cord to get your dog into the crate.) This exercise is "Stimulus-Command-Response," so you will turn on the stimulation before giving your dog the "Kennel" command, then follow immediately with the command itself.

Give the command just once. Keep the continuous stimulation on until the dog is completely in the crate, then turn it off immediately. Timing is critical: Release the button as soon as your dog's rear end has passed through the open door. If he freezes or balks at going into the kennel, you must use the check cord to pull him to it and force him inside within ten seconds. You don't want your dog to make the association that by gritting his teeth for 10.1 seconds he can turn off the stimulation. Quite the opposite; you want him to understand that going into the kennel causes the stimulation to end, that he can turn it off by obeying your command. You are teaching him that his kennel is a sanctuary, a safe zone. This is an important concept for your dog to learn, and it's one that you will use in other aspects of training.

Let me emphasize again that timing is of the utmost importance in all E-collar work. This means that when teaching the "Kennel" command, *never apply stimulation when your dog is in the crate*. If your pup refuses to come out when you call him, pull him to you by his collar or with the check cord. If you apply stimulation in the kennel and the dog associates the pressure with what he thought was a safe place, he will obviously be confused. This, in turn, will create a lack of confidence and, thus, adversely affect the dog's style.

I can't tell you how many repetitions of this exercise your dog will require. Some learn quickly that obeying your command will turn off the stimulation, while others need more time. A sure-fire indicator that your dog understands how to remove the pressure is that he runs into the kennel as soon as he feels the stimulation, anticipating your verbal command. Once your dog knows that he can turn off stimulation himself, it is much easier for him to learn how to avoid it altogether.

Avoiding stimulation is what your pup will learn in the third stage, "Command-Stimulus-Response." Now, with a check cord on the dog, give the "Kennel" command first— again, just once—followed by stimulation *only if your pup does not obey.* In the initial stage of "Command-Stimulus-Response," start off close to the kennel, say six to eight feet away. Give the command "Kennel." If your dog does not obey within a second, hit the button, and leave the stimulation on until he goes into the kennel. Note, however, that timing is important. There must be a short delay between your giving the command and your pressing the button. If the two occur simultaneously, your dog will have no opportunity to learn to "beat" the stimulation. By teaching him that he can avoid it by promptly obeying your command, you will create a bold, enthusiastic partner.

Once your dog is 100 percent reliable at a distance of eight feet from the kennel, you can move him farther away before giving the command. But don't jump from eight feet away to sixty feet and expect success. Gradually increase the distance—moving beyond eight feet in three-foot increments. That way, your dog will handle the learning curve much more easily.

As before, you should always give the command first, followed by stimulation if your pup doesn't obey. The only change as you increase the distance past eight feet is to turn off the stimulation *as soon as the dog moves toward the kennel.* If he deviates after that point, hit the button again until he is back on track, heading for the kennel. For example, if your dog is ten yards from the kennel when you give the command and he does not obey, put the stimulation on and leave it on until he heads in the right direction. When this happens, immediately turn the stimulation off. But if he moves out, say, five yards from your side and decides not to continue, immediately reapply the stimulation, and leave it on until he heads toward the kennel again. *At no time during this process should you give the "Kennel" command a second time.*

With enough repetitions, you should be able to send your dog directly into the kennel from a distance of twenty yards. This exercise will show him that he can avoid—and thus control—the electronic stimulation. In the process, there will be a boost in his confidence and style. Once your dog is entering the crate immediately upon hearing "Kennel" (thus avoiding stimulation), you are in the final, "Command-Response" stage.

At this point, you can move on to teaching the remaining basic commands—"Sit," "Here," and "Heel"—using electronic stimulation. The methods and stages are precisely the same as those you just used for the "Kennel" command.

To introduce "Sit," you should start with plenty of "Show Pups," as described in Chapter 4. Your dog must absolutely know what the command "Sit" means before the electronics are brought into play. Once the "Show Pup" stage has been completed, put the pup on a check cord, and apply his predetermined level of stimulation, followed immediately by the command, "Sit." When the dog's posterior hits the ground, immediately turn off the stimulation. If he refuses to sit, you must force the issue by pushing his rump down within ten seconds (remember, after this period the stimulation will turn off automatically).

Once your dog starts to sit as soon as you apply the stimulation—even before you give the verbal command—you'll know that he understands how to turn off the pressure. You are now ready to teach him how to *avoid* the stimulation by advancing to the "Command-Stimulus-Response" stage. Here again, it is advisable to have your dog on a check cord, because you want to make sure he does not escape the lesson by running away. Give the command "Sit" first, followed by stimulation if the dog does not obey immediately. Again, you must make him sit within the ten-second duration of the stimulation cycle. As with "Kennel," when your dog is consistently sitting upon hearing the verbal command "Sit," you are in the final, "Command-Response" stage. At any time thereafter, if you give the command and the dog does not sit, apply stimulation until he obeys. With enough repetition of this drill, sitting immediately will become a conditioned response.

To incorporate the whistle into "Sit," simply give one short blast on the whistle, followed by the verbal command. (This is the pre-cue/cue method introduced in Chapter 7.) If your pup does not obey, apply stimulation until he is sitting. With enough repetitions of the whistle blast followed immediately by the verbal command, the dog will anticipate the verbal command and will sit upon hearing the whistle. At this point, it is time to demand excellence in your pup's response to the whistle command. Give the blast with no voice command. If the dog sits, walk up to him and praise him. If he does not obey, apply the stimulation, and leave the stimulation on until he is sitting.

Although your pup should now be fully and instantly obeying the verbal and/or whistle command to sit, he has been worked close to you—on a check cord— and has been under your immediate control. That may be as far as you wish to take remote training of the "Sit" command. If you choose to use electronics to extend the distance at which the dog will sit, you can do so by continuing the drills I've described while gradually working the dog farther and farther away. I suggest keeping your pup on a check cord until you can confidently wager your life savings that he will sit on command off the check cord. For anything beyond these exercises, it would be wise to consult a manual specializing in intermediate and advanced electronic training.

To teach "Here," first demonstrate what the command means with "Show Pups," pulling him to you on a check cord while repeating "Here," "Here," "Here." Once you are sure your dog knows what the command means, move to "Stimulus-Command-Response." With the dog still on a check cord and sitting six to eight feet away, apply the stimulation, give the "Here" command once, and immediately pull him to you. When he reaches you, release the button.

Once your pup begins to come to you upon feeling the stimulation—even before hearing the command—graduate to "Command-Stimulus-Response." Keeping the dog on a check cord, issue the verbal command *one time*. If he comes, give him a "Good boy" or "Attaboy." If he balks at the command, apply stimulation until he comes. As in teaching "Kennel," when you are working the dog beyond eight feet, turn off the stimulation as soon as he starts coming to you.

If your pup is ten yards away when you command "Here" and he tests you by not obeying, apply stimulation. As soon as he starts coming, release the button. Give him plenty of praise when he gets to you.

To incorporate the whistle into "Here," follow the same procedure as in teaching "Sit." I use a continuous trill for my recall command, though as I said in Chapter 6, some trainers favor four distinct blasts. With your pup on a check cord, blow the whistle and follow it with the verbal command. If the dog does not respond, apply stimulation until he obeys. Once again, with enough repetitions your flusher will understand that the verbal command immediately follows the trill of the whistle, and ultimately, he will recall on the whistle alone. At this point, if you give the whistle command and the dog responds, praise him. If he does not obey, turn on the stimulation until he starts toward you.

In teaching "Here," it is possible that your dog may develop a reluctance to leave your side, primarily because he gets electronic stimulation when he's away from you and fails to respond quickly to the recall command. One of the reasons that I teach "Kennel" before "Here" is to give me the means to quickly remedy this situation. If your dog does become stuck to your side, mix in a few kennel exercises to remind him that leaving you can be a positive experience.

To teach "Heel," you must first go through numerous "Show Pups," as described above. Once the dog clearly understands what the command means (without your demanding obedience), move on to "Stimulus-Command-Response." Walking with your dog on a lead, turn on his predetermined level of stimulation, give the command "Heel" *once*, and pull him to your side. When the dog's head is by your knee, turn off the stimulation.

Because you can't walk in a straight line forever, you will have to teach your pup to turn with you when he is heeling. At first, make gradual, wide turns so he can stay keyed on your leg, which is his guidepost. If he begins to wander during a turn, apply stimulation and pull him back to your leg. *Do not repeat the "Heel" command.* As soon as his head is at your knee, turn off the stimulation. When he begins to understand that he must stay beside your knee—wherever it leads him—start shortening your turns, changing directions, and walking in circles and figure eights.

As with all training exercises, continue these drills during short sessions, rather than hour-long marathons. Once your dog heels immediately upon feeling stimulation, your side has become another safe zone, and you can advance to the "Command-Stimulus-Response" stage.

Again, while walking your pup on lead, give the command "Heel" one time. If he obeys, praise him. If he does not obey, apply stimulation continuously until he is heeling properly. Remember to continue your turning drills. You can anticipate some disobedience at first, and the proper response is to apply stimulation until he is at your side.

Before you advance to heeling your pup off-lead, he must be obeying the "Heel" command perfectly when he is under your control on-lead. If he isn't fully reliable when attached to you by six feet of stout leather or nylon, be assured that his responses will be much worse off-lead. The same thing goes for other niceties of advanced heel training, such as heeling from a distance, backing up, and making sharp, snappy turns when at heel. Whether you decide to advance to this level of performance or not, give your pup a firm grounding with the basic "Heel" command as I've described and you will have a dog that, at the very least, will walk at your side in a controlled manner.

Once you have taught your dog the four commands using electronic stimulation in the above manner, he has been properly introduced to the collar. He has learned how to turn off stimulation and, subsequently, how to avoid it altogether by obeying your command the first time you issue it. Even if you never use the electronic collar for anything other than teaching the four yard commands, this tool will—in my opinion—help you to produce a better all-around gun dog, one that responds to all levels of training enthusiastically and reliably. In addition, if you are going to incorporate electronics into all aspects of your field training program (as I do), it is mandatory that you first correctly teach your dog the fundamentals of stimulation as I have already described.

Whether in the yard or the field, low-level electronic stimulation presents your dog with a problem that he cannot solve by running away, biting, or sulking. In the program presented here, he overcomes this problem by obeying your commands, then he learns that he can avoid the pressure completely by obeying immediately. And, being a dog—a creature of habit and positive associations—he will stick with what works for him.

Again, however, the electronic collar is not a device that allows you to shortcut the training process. With or without the collar, you must go through certain stages and repetitions. Remote electronics are simply hands-off aids that help you reinforce and expand on commands that your dog already understands. Any other use of these devices amounts to punishment training, and it will not create a stylish, confident, controlled flushing dog.

Appendix C: The Conditioned Retrieve

First, let me say that neither Joe Arnette nor I would buy a retriever or spaniel puppy out of parents that did not exhibit a powerful desire to retrieve. Nor would we want a puppy from an otherwise excellent repeat breeding if the dogs from the first litter did not show strong retrieving instincts. In other words, retrieving should be genetically instilled in upland flushing dogs, and they should exhibit a tremendous desire to fetch birds. That said, even pups of excellent breeding will need further training if they are to achieve true excellence as retrievers.

The conditioned—or forced—retrieve (often referred to as "force-fetching") is not a fun or easy part of training, and I advise you not to try it unless you have the time, patience, and understanding to complete the process. If you do make the commitment to the conditioned retrieve, you *must* finish it. Stopping in midstream often produces undesirable results that will show up in other stages of training. If your flushing dog retrieves in a manner that you consider adequate, and if game he delivers is fit for consumption (in other words, the birds are not mangled), you may decide that the conditioned retrieve is unnecessary.

Having said that, I must tell you that I put every one of my dogs through conditioned-retrieve training because it yields many benefits beyond producing a flusher that will retrieve every time, all the time. Experience has proven repeatedly that the process of the conditioned retrieve makes the dog a better student in all aspects of training.

As we have noted before, your dog is a pack animal. Once he has completed the conditioned-retrieve program, he will understand absolutely that you are the leader of the pack. In addition, he will know that you are going to give each command just one time and that you expect obedience. When it has been ingrained in your flusher, this knowledge will produce a bold, enthusiastic learner and a confident gun dog. If a pup is timid, the conditioned retrieve will often make him bolder and more sure of himself. A dog that is a case-hardened rebel will also benefit from the process, becoming more cooperative in training and developing into a better companion.

The conditioned retrieve will often cure hard-mouth, as well as teach an overly soft-mouthed dog to deliver professionally and to hold the bird until given the command to release it. Once you have taught your dog the conditioned retrieve, the command to fetch a bird is no longer a request. It is no different than "Sit" or "Here," and nothing short of excellence will be tolerated.

As in most aspects of dog training, there are different approaches to the conditioned retrieve. I am going to describe the methods I use, but it will be up to you to decide on the right program for you and your dog. (See the bibliography for additional sources of information on this subject.) As a rule of thumb, I would say that any dog under eight months of age is too young to go through the process of the conditioned retrieve. I like to begin after a dog has been shot over, and my decision about when to start the process may hinge on his performance in the field. If he goes for a retrieve but won't pick up the bird or plays with it, crushes it, or tries to eat it, I will elect to teach him the conditioned retrieve before continuing field work.

With other dogs, I sometimes complete one hunting season and do the conditioned retrieve during the winter months, when bird work is difficult. If I encounter a dog that has a natural retrieving instinct but a sloppy delivery—say, he drags his birds by the wing—I usually begin the conditioned retrieve before I progress to steadiness training. The same is true for an otherwise decent retriever that is hard-mouthed. If a dog retrieves and does *not* exhibit such problems, I normally start the conditioned retrieve after refining basic yard commands, as described in Chapter 7, but prior to the steadying work that was covered in Chapter 8.

Equipment is a key factor in the conditioned retrieve, and a sturdy training table, or bench, with a splinter-free, nonskid top is most important of all. Mine measures sixteen feet long and twenty-four inches wide, and it is about waist-high. There is a vertical post at each end (on the centerline), and a cable stretches from the top of one upright to the top of the other. I rig a pulley on this cable, equipping it with a short length of chain and a snap for the dog's collar. This way, a pup can run the length of the bench but is unable to jump off it. Firmly secured to one of the posts is a standard, buckle-type collar.

Before beginning formal conditioned-retrieve training, I want the dog to be completely comfortable on the bench.

So, whenever possible, I put the pup on the table and play with him, give him biscuits, and generally get him used to running up and down on this new surface. In the beginning, at least, I want him to think that the table is a good place. Simply tying the dog to one of the uprights and starting force training would be very counterproductive.

However, when your pup is accustomed to the bench and enthusiastically runs the length of the cable, you are ready to begin serious training. Start by securing the dog's head to the post that's equipped with the collar. I also attach Velcro straps to the table and wrap these around his hind legs to prevent him from twisting from side to side in his attempt to escape. In addition, I throw a half-hitch around his belly and run the line up to the overhead cable. With the dog essentially immobilized, the force training will go much more easily.

When you first secure your pup's head, belly, and rear

Use a half-hitch or slip knot (shown) to secure the dog's midsection, running the line up to the table's overhead cable.

legs, he will probably struggle and try to pull away. In your initial sessions, the goal is simply to get the dog accustomed to being restrained—to the point that he stops fighting his immobility. This may take five minutes, or it may take five days. I treat the conditioned retrieve as if I have all the time in the world, with no expectations. It is a mistake to assume that you are going to accomplish Step A on day one and Step B on day two.

Here is another rule of thumb: It will take you four to eight weeks to complete the conditioned retrieve, and it is your pup's behavior that will tell you when to advance from one stage to the next. It is important that you *never* let the dog think that he has won a battle on the training table. If at some point he refuses to cooperate and you decide to quit and try again tomorrow, the next session will be harder, not easier. In teaching the conditioned retrieve, *you* must win every battle. If your dog even suspects that he has the upper hand, he will only become tougher and will fight you every step of the way in future training.

Once your dog is no longer struggling when restrained, proceed with the toe hitch. I use this technique—rather than the common ear pinch—because I do not want my hand near the dog's mouth. (I have never been bitten and would like to keep that record intact.) To form a toe hitch, take a piece of line (sash cord works well), and tie a half-hitch or a slip knot at one end. Don't use a line so thin that it will cut into his skin. Attach the cord to one of the dog's front legs, positioning it above the paw and first joint. Do *not* put the toe hitch on his left leg one day and his right leg another day. You want to establish a consistent point of contact.

With the slip knot secured just above the joint, so that it cannot slide down, run the line behind the dog's leg, under his outside toe, over his two middle toes, and back under the other outside toe. (Placing the line over just one toe will exert more pressure, but you run the risk of wrenching the toe.) Then take the tag end and slip it between the dog's leg and the line that's running down the back of the leg (see below). That way, when you step back and pull on the cord, it puts pressure on the two inner toes; when you stop pulling, the pressure is released.

The proper way to form the toe hitch

In addition to the training table and toe hitch, you'll need a wooden dowel about twelve inches long and one inch in diameter. If you start the conditioned retrieve with a training dummy or, especially, a bird and make a mistake, you may create a retrieving problem with real game. But if a problem arises with the dowel and the dog no longer wants to pick one up, so be it. Wrap your dowel with twine so that if he bites it, he won't get splinters in his mouth.

Now, with your pup completely restrained on the table and with the toe hitch in place, pull steadily on the cord—

hard enough to hurt the dog. When he opens his mouth to yelp, quickly insert the dowel into it, and immediately release the toe hitch. The concept is that when the dowel is in his mouth, his toes no longer hurt. This is a process of conditioned association. At first, your dog will probably spit out the dowel when the pain ends. When he does, reapply the pressure and reinsert the dowel into his mouth.

It will take a number of repetitions before your dog learns that when he holds the dowel, there is no pressure on his toes. Remember, experiences that are either very negative or very positive are quickly imprinted on a dog's mind. This does not mean that he will always accept the dowel readily—only that he has made the association. I can't tell you how many repetitions it will take before your dog will consistently hold the dowel in his mouth. That depends on the individual dog.

In the initial stages of teaching the conditioned retrieve, once the dog is holding the dowel for three to five seconds, I take it out of his mouth. If your pup is reluctant to release the dowel, you may have to roll it back toward the juncture of his upper and lower jaws while forcing his mouth open with your other hand. Do *not* play tug-of-war with the dog; it is important to get the dowel out quickly and efficiently. However, at this stage, do not give him a release command such as "Give," "Drop," or "Leave it." Your sole focus now should be teaching the dog to hold the dowel; you will introduce a release command separately, at a later date.

When introducing your pup to the conditioned retrieve, short sessions are preferable to long ones. I would much rather do three five-minute lessons on the training table than one fifteen-minute exercise. At Grouse Wing, we put dogs on the bench six to eight times a day, because short, repetitive sessions work best.

In the beginning, the process does not involve your pup's reaching for the dowel, nor his responding to a command, such as "Hold" or "Fetch." Let me review the sequence: You apply pressure on the toe hitch, and when your pup opens his mouth to yelp, you insert the dowel, and release the hitch. Eventually, the dog will understand how to "turn off" the stimulation, just as he did in the drills aimed at refining his response to yard commands. Once your pup is consistently holding the dowel, you can move to the next step: teaching him to reach for it.

With the dog strapped to the upright, place the dowel a couple of inches from his mouth and pull on the toe hitch. This time, do not put the dowel into his mouth—make him take it out of your hand. By continuing to pull on his toes, you will force him to reach out for the dowel. Now you need to give the dog the ability to move his head a bit more. One way to do that is to loop the post's collar not around

At a point in training, your dog should reach out and take the dowel or, as in this photo, a training dummy.

your pup's neck but through his own flat collar. Now, gradually increase the distance at which you present the dowel, moving from three inches to perhaps a foot in small increments. At some time in the process, you will no longer have to pull hard on your dog's toes. Just a small amount of pressure will prompt him to reach out and take the dowel.

Some dogs accept the dowel quickly, while others fight it extremely hard. Don't think you're doing something wrong if your dog does not take the dowel and hold it in the first five minutes. This may require a couple of days or even a week, though some dogs do, indeed, respond almost immediately. Just keep moving along, going step by step. Once your dog reaches out and takes the dowel from several inches away *every time,* you are ready to introduce a verbal command.

Until now, the cue for your dog to take the dowel has been pressure on his toes, but it is now time to introduce a pre-cue. Give the command "Hold," which at this point means nothing to the dog, and immediately pull on the toe hitch. He will take the dowel to shut off the stimulation, just as he has done before. With enough repetitions, he will anticipate that the toe hitch is going to follow the verbal command. At that point, he will start taking the dowel as soon as he hears "Hold"—*before* you pull on the cord. In other words, he will learn that he can avoid pressure by complying with the command.

So far, your pup has remained strapped to the upright during this entire process. Once he consistently takes the dowel on the "Hold" command and knows how to beat the pain of the toe hitch, you are ready to release the belly line and unstrap the dog's rear legs. Although his head remains secured to the upright, he will have fewer restraints than previously. Present the dowel and give the command

"Hold." If he takes it, give him an "Attaboy." If he refuses, pull on the toe hitch until he reaches out and grabs the dowel. Once the dog will reliably reach out and take it *every time* that you say "Hold," you are ready to integrate the electronic collar into the process.

The reason for making the transition to electronic stimulation is that eventually you will take the dog off the bench and work with him on the ground. There, with the collar, you can correct him easily and immediately if he does not obey. However, you cannot use one of these devices from the outset in the conditioned retrieve because, as I explained in Appendix B, most of them turn off automatically after a set time (usually ten seconds). If, in the early stages of the force training, you applied electronic stimulation and your pup refused to open his mouth, the stimulation might shut itself off, giving the dog the impression that he had won the battle.

He would perceive that simply by gritting his teeth and keeping his mouth shut, he could prevail. The dog would become tougher, and your problems would be magnified. By contrast, with the toe hitch, you can exert pressure for as long as it takes to get the dog to yelp, giving you the opportunity to put the dowel into his mouth. The same is true for teaching the "Hold" command; even if your dog fights for more than ten seconds, you are able to keep the pressure on his toes until he takes the dowel. This is important.

In order to make the transition to the E-collar in the conditioned retrieve, you must again use the concept of pre-cue/cue. In addition, you must first thoroughly accustom the dog to the collar and establish the appropriate minimum stimulation level following the procedures described in Appendix B.

Thus far, the cue for your pup to take the dowel has

been pressure on his toes. Therefore, apply the electronic stimulation, then immediately pull on the toe hitch. At first, the dog will take the dowel because of the toe-hitch cue, not in response to the pre-cue of electronic stimulation. But, as you repeat this exercise, he will anticipate that whenever he feels the stimulation, the toe hitch will quickly follow. Then, he will start to take the dowel on the stimulation alone.

Now, reintroduce the command "Hold." If he takes the dowel in response, praise him. If he does not, apply electronic stimulation until he reaches for it. Don't rush this stage. You want to be sure that he's reliable and does not fight the stimulation for ten seconds. Once the dog is religious on the "Hold" command, it's time to unstrap him from the upright.

Understand that because he is no longer fully restrained (though he's still clipped to the cable and pulley), your pup may feel that you are no longer in control. He may balk. Present the dowel a couple of inches in front of his muzzle, and give the command "Hold." If he takes the dowel, give him a pat and an "Attaboy." If he does not, apply stimulation until he obeys. Then, in small steps, move the dowel farther away each time. You want him to move to get it— first from inches away, then from one foot, then two feet, then three feet until he'll run the length of the bench to get the dowel. By this time, he should be holding it until you virtually have to pry it out of his mouth. You have not yet introduced a release command. That will come later.

While your pup is holding the dowel, tap it with your hand. He should not release it. The reason for this exercise is that if you always take the dowel when you put your hand up to his mouth, that act will become a cue for him to drop it. Later, when he's retrieving a crippled bird and you reach down to take it, he may spit it out and the bird may escape. As I just said, you will teach the release command separately. For now, you want to tap and pull on the dowel frequently to ensure that your pup maintains his hold on it.

At this point, the dog should sit and hold the dowel for at least five minutes. If he drops it, put it in front of his face and turn the stimulation back on until he takes it. Once your flusher will religiously hold the dowel and will move down the length of the bench to take it, you're ready to move to the next step.

Once you have reached this stage of the conditioned retrieve, you can extend the length of each session—but not by much. Short, frequent lessons are still best, though the dog should be able to handle training for five to ten minutes at a time. End each session on a positive note, praising the dog with an appreciative "Good boy" when he gets and holds the dowel as he should.

Now hold the dowel a bit lower down and give the command "Hold." When the dog learns to reach down and take it from a distance of six inches, go to eight inches and then to ten inches—until the dowel is resting on the table as you hold it. Next, you are going to let go of the dowel and tell your pup to pick it up. To date, however, your hand has always been part of the conditioned-retrieve process, so recognize that when you take your hand away, the dog may fail. *Always proceed in small steps.*

Once your dog will consistently reach down and pick up the dowel from the table while you're holding it, pull your hand back a couple of inches. Give the command "Hold." When he succeeds in that, draw your hand back a couple more inches. When he can handle that, gradually put the dowel farther away until your dog will take it quickly from a distance of one foot, then two feet, and so on. Keep this up until you can give the command "Hold" and he will run down the entire length of the table to pick up the dowel. At this point, you want to be upbeat. Make the process a game, and offer plenty of praise—"All right!" and "Attaboy!" If at any point your dog fails to pick up the dowel, turn on the electronic stimulation until he succeeds.

After a period of time, your dog should run the length of the table to pick up a dowel or dummy and return it to you.

Once the dog regularly goes up and down the bench to pick up the dowel, you can move to the ground. I would suggest, however, that you start in a closed-in area, like a garage. You may want to keep a check cord on the dog, too.

Begin by telling your pup to sit. Present the dowel in front of his muzzle, and give the command "Hold." If he does not take it, apply electronic stimulation until he obeys. Do *not* repeat the command. As always, you are training your dog to comply the first time around. Once he is sitting, taking the dowel, and holding it in his mouth, you can lower it several inches below his face. Command "Hold," and see that he bends his neck to take it. As before, gradually move the dowel closer and closer to the ground. Again, when you first lay the dowel on the ground, continue to hold onto it. Then, gradually move your hand farther and farther from the dowel until the dog will consistently reach down and pick it up without needing your hand as a cue.

At this point, I suggest you move to an area of mowed grass, where you and the dog can easily see the dowel. Toss it out about a foot in front of him, and command "Hold." He should move quickly to get it. If he doesn't, apply electronic stimulation until he obeys, but do not repeat the command. Gradually increase the distance you are throwing the dowel until your pup will consistently run thirty or forty feet to pick it up. Once he has reached this level of achievement, return to the training table for the introduction of birds.

Just as you did in the beginning, secure the dog's head to the post equipped with the collar, harness his belly, and restrain his hind legs in the Velcro straps. Reattach the toe hitch. Before you give your pup birds, I recommend that you first introduce other objects for him to hold—a tennis ball, a sock, a glove. Follow exactly the same procedure you initially used with the dowel; the dog should begin accepting and holding the new objects in a matter of just a few sessions. He simply needs to know that the command "Hold" applies to anything that's presented to him.

Once your pup is responding to the toe hitch in this exercise, move to the E-collar and electronic stimulation, just as you did in teaching the dog to take and hold the dowel. Then, when he is clearly comfortable with a variety of objects, you can move on to a bird.

Start with a lock-wing pigeon. Pull on the toe hitch and when your pup yelps, insert the bird into his mouth. If he spits it out, reapply the pressure on his toes. Once he consistently accepts and holds the bird, present it several inches in front of his face and pull on the toe hitch until he reaches out and takes it. When the dog responds consistently, make the transition from the toe hitch to the E-collar, as you did before. From here on out, the procedure is identical to that you used when you first taught "Hold" with the dowel; simply follow all the same steps. As soon as your pup will consistently run the length of the table, pick up the bird, and bring it back, you are ready to go to the ground.

For this stage in the process, it will be helpful if you return to a retrieving corridor (page 85), which will ensure that the dog brings the bird to you, rather than running away with it. Using a check cord will give you additional control. If your pup is line steady, command "Sit," then toss out a clipwing. Give the command "Hold" to send him for it. If you have a check cord on the dog, you can guide him back to you as you give the command "Here." If he drops the bird, turn on the electronic stimulation until he picks it up. When the dog is performing reliably under these controlled conditions, you can move beyond the retrieving corridor.

Start with short tosses in a mowed area—just as you did with the dowel—until the dog will eagerly and consistently fetch a clip-wing or Velcro-restrained pigeon thrown a distance of thirty feet or so. Now you can make the transition to sending your pup on his name. Let's say the dog's name is Rufus. Sit him down at heel, throw the clipwing, and give the pre-cue/cue: "Rufus, Hold." At first, the dog will leave on the "Hold" part of the command, but with enough repetitions he will make the association and leave on his name. At that point, you can drop the command "Hold" and send him on his name alone. I see this as a big advantage, because if I am hunting two dogs trained to pick up a bird on "Hold" or "Fetch," both will leave when I give that command. By making the transition to using their names, only the dog I have chosen for the retrieve will respond, thus avoiding a battle over the bird.

Once your pup is reliably fetching pigeons, you should return to the training table and introduce him to pheasants.

Don't assume that because your dog will reliably pick up pigeons that he will do the same with pheasants. You must train him to hold a larger bird.

You cannot assume that because the dog is reliable on pigeons he will be consistent on these much larger birds. You'll have to train him to hold them, but it will take only a short time. Repeat the same steps you used when starting him on pigeons, but use a freshly killed pheasant so that your dog is more inclined to accept it. When he is eagerly reaching for the bird, demand that he hold it for several minutes.

Up to this point, you have simply been taking the dowel, dummy, pigeon, or pheasant out of your pup's mouth when he retrieves it. Now, however, you're going to teach him the command to give you the object. Put your dog back on the bench (immobilizing him should no longer be necessary), and have him hold a pigeon. Now say "Drop," Give," or "Leave"—whatever you decide to use as a release command—and take the bird from his mouth, giving him an "Attaboy" and a pat. After you have done this a number of times, your pup will associate that the command "Give" means to let go of the bird.

In the early stages of learning the release command, the dog may be reluctant to give up the bird. Remember, up to now, good things have happened when he has held on to an object, and bad things have happened when he has refused to accept it or has dropped it. So, be patient with your pup. If he doesn't respond when you give the release command, pinch his upper lip against his incisors. When he gives you the bird, praise him immediately. With enough repititions, the dog should release the bird readily. If at any time he drops it or holds it too loosely, apply electronic stimulation until he picks up the bird and grasps it properly with his mouth.

Once you finish teaching your dog the conditioned retrieve, you will have a flusher that fetches birds and dummies enthusiastically every time. And, as I said at the beginning of this appendix, your pup will respond better to all aspects of training. Do not anthropomorphize and think, "I wouldn't like my toes hurt and wouldn't love somebody who did it to me." Your dog is a pack animal, and once he understands his subordinate position in your pack, he will accept it. He is fully capable of learning how to solve problems like avoiding the toe hitch and the electronic stimulation by complying with your command the first time. Moreover, if you remain upbeat and consistent in training the conditioned retrieve, you and your dog will emerge from the process a stronger, more effective team, and that will pay big dividends in the field.

Selected Bibliography

As I said in the Introduction, there are a good many gun-dog training books on the market. And, in addition to publications devoted to hunting dogs, there are even greater numbers that describe how to select, care for, and train personal (companion) dogs. Although the latter group of books doesn't deal specifically with flushing breeds, that does not mean the material presented is valueless. Quite the contrary. Some "companion-dog" books are well written and contain a wealth of information rarely offered to gun-dog owners. There is nothing wrong with using selected tidbits of wisdom that you might find in these books. That said, here is some cautionary advice:

Except in the early stages, the training of a companion dog differs from the training that a flushing dog must receive to do his job properly. On the whole, you should stick with the approach that George Hickox and I have presented and not deviate to a companion-dog-training program that sounds easier but cannot give your pup what he requires.

Use what you can from these sources, but use it judiciously.

The following bibliography represents what George and I believe are the better books, specialty magazines, videos, and websites available to expand your knowledge of dogs and their behavior and training. Some of the selections are annotated to clarify their content beyond what the title offers.

—*Joe Arnette*

Books

Bauman, Diane. *Beyond Basic Dog Training.* New York: Howell Book House, 1987.

Benjamin, Carol Lea. *Mother Knows Best: The Natural Way to Train Your Dog.* New York: Howell Book House, 1985. (This is one of the top companion-dog training books on the market. It is a nicely written blend of common sense and canine behavior.)

Bergler, Reinhold. *Man and Dog: The Psychology of a Relationship.* New York: Howell Book House, 1988.

Carlson, Delbert G., and James M. Griffin. *Dog Owner's Home Veterinary Handbook.* New York: Howell Book House, 1989. (This is a comprehensive health guide to help dog owners avoid and/or deal with emergencies and day-to-day problems.)

Carlton, H. W. *Spaniels: Their Breaking for Sport and Field Trials.* London: The Field & Queen Ltd., 1915. (This is the classic British training book. One of the most influential manuals written in the twentieth century, it is, however, dated in its techniques and style.)

Collins, Donald R. *The Collins Guide to Dog Nutrition*. New York: Howell Book House, 1987 (Revised).

Dobbs, Jim, et al. *Tri-Tronics Retriever Training*. Tucson: Tri-Tronics Inc., 1993. (This is by far the most comprehensive and detailed book currently available on training retrievers with remote electronics.)

Erlandson, Keith. *Gun Dog Training*. London: Popular Dogs Publishing Co. Ltd., 1976.

_____. *The Working Springer Spaniel*. London: Robinson Publishing Co., 1995.

Fox, Michael W. *Understanding Your Dog*. New York: Coward, McCann and Geoghegan, 1974. (Dr. Fox offers a sound introduction to the evolutionary, psychological, and physiological roots of canine behavior.)

_____. *How to be Your Pet's Best Friend*. New York: Coward, McCann and Geoghegan, 1981.

Free, James Lamb. *Training Your Retriever*. New York: Coward, McCann and Geoghegan,1949. (Free's lively book remains the American classic on training non-slip retrievers with traditional methods. Some of his advice is dated.)

George, Bobby N. *Training Retrievers: The Cotton Pershall Method*. Traverse City, MI: Countrysport Press, 1990. (Few retriever trainers have been as influential as Cotton Pershall, and Bobby George has done a creditable job presenting his techniques.)

Irving, Joe. *Training Spaniels*. North Pomfret, VT: David & Charles Inc., 1980.

_____. *Gundogs, Their Learning Chain*. London: A&C Black Ltd., 1983.

Lopez, Barry Holstun. *Of Wolves and Men*. New York: Charles Scribner's Sons, 1978. (A rich and intelligently written popular account of wolf biology and the animal's interaction with humans.)

Lorenz, Conrad. *Man Meets Dog*. New York: Kodansha America, 1953.

McLoughlin, John C. *The Canine Clan: a New Look at Man's Best Friend*. New York: Viking Press, 1983.

Mech, L. David. *The Wolf: The Ecology and Behavior of an Endangered Species*. Garden City; Doubleday, 1970.

Monks of New Skete. *How to be Your Dog's Best Friend*. Boston: Little Brown & Co., 1978. (If I had to pick just two books dealing with all aspects of developing a first-class companion dog, they would be this one and its follow-up volume, *The Art of Raising a Puppy*.)

_____*The Art of Raising a Puppy*. Boston: Little Brown & Co., 1991. (This book has a section on puppy-evaluation tests and their relevance to owners.)

Pfaffenberger, Clarence. *The New Knowledge of Dog Behavior*. New York: Howell Book House, 1963. (Pfaffenberger was one of the first researchers to develop and expand puppy-evaluation tests and their interpretation.)

Radcliffe, Talbot. *Spaniels for Sport*. London: Faber and Faber, 1969. (This book is a follow-up to H. W. Carlton's British classic, listed previously. Radcliffe was one of the twentieth century's primary breeders and trainers of working spaniels.)

Roebuck, Kenneth C. *Gun Dog Training Spaniels and Retrievers*. Harrisburg: Stackpole Books, 1982.

Serpell, James (ed.). *The Domestic Dog: Its Evolution, Behavior, and Interactions with People*. Cambridge, Great Britain: University Press, 1995. (Serpell has put together a unique book based on a scholarly "natural history" of the domestic dog and its position in human society.)

Whitney, Leon F. *Dog Psychology: The Basis of Dog Training*. New York: Howell Book House. 1964, 1971.

Wolters, Richard A. *The Labrador Retriever: The History . . . The People. . . . Revisited*. New York: Penguin Books. 1981, 1992.

NOTE: Most of the primary flushing and retrieving breeds have specific books devoted to their history. Generally, these breed books focus on show animals and their lineage, but they will provide a broad look at an individual breed of dog. They are available at most book or pet-supply stores. Also, The American Kennel Club offers revised and updated editions of *The Complete Dog Book,* which describes every breed of dog recognized at the time of publication.

Specialty Magazines

Three specialty gun-dog magazines are among the best, up-to-date, regular sources of information for trainers and upland-bird hunters at all skill levels. They differ from generic outdoor publications because of their tight focus on hunting dogs. The three selections offer a wealth of knowledge and are an excellent source of breeders, trainers, training books and videos, and equipment. These publications are staffed and written by knowledgeable dog people. Anyone involved with working gun dogs should subscribe to at least one of these magazines. Which one depends on your broader interests and what you want from a publication.

Gun Dog Magazine, P.O. Box 35098, Des Moines, IA 50315; (515) 243-2472. (*Gun Dog* is the oldest, most respected, and widely read of the North American hunting-dog magazines. Although it does not emphasize any one particular working style of gun dog over another, the magazine provides a regular "Flush" column and numerous feature articles on training flushing dogs.)

The Retriever Journal, P.O. Box 968, Traverse City, MI 49685; (800) 272-3246. (*The Retriever Journal,* as it name indicates, focuses on working retrievers, though spaniel-based articles run periodically. The magazine's primary thrust is toward non-slip retrievers, but it also offers a range of information on most subjects dealing with retrievers, including upland flushing work.)

Spaniels in the Field, 10714 Escondido Dr., Cincinnati, OH 45249; (513) 489-2727. (*Spaniels in the Field* is the only North American publication devoted strictly to hunting (not show or bench) spaniels. It covers their training and use as field-trial and wingshooting dogs. The magazine's emphasis tends toward springer spaniels simply because of that breed's numerical dominance in the field.)

Videos

NOTE: These tapes are available in the "bookshelf" section of most of the listed gun-dog magazines and through most gun-dog-supply outfits.

An Introduction to the Electronic Dog-Training Collar. Featuring Bob West and Roger Sparks. Running Time: 28 minutes.

Gun Dog Training Spaniels. Featuring Kenneth C. Roebuck. Running Time: 90 Minutes.

Pheasants and Labs. Featuring George Hickox, with shooting tips from Michael MacIntosh. Running time: 85 minutes.

Top Dog. (Training advanced hunting retrievers using the electronic collar.) Featuring Tony Hartnett. Running time: 78 minutes.

The Trained Retrieve. Featuring Bob West and Roger Sparks. Running Time: 26 Minutes.

Trained Retrieve, Part I "Hold." Featuring Jim & Phyllis Dobbs. Running Time: 70 Minutes. And, *Trained Retrieve, Part II "Fetch."* Featuring Jim & Phyllis Dobbs. Running Time: 60 Minutes. (If you intend to force-fetch your flusher, watch both tapes before beginning.)

Training The Upland Flushing Dog. Tape 1. Featuring George Hickox. Running Time: 45 Minutes.

Training The Upland Flushing Dog. Tape 2. Featuring George Hickox. Running Time: 45 Minutes.

Websites

NOTE: More of these are appearing and improving almost daily, but here are two that are certainly worth frequent visits.

www.working-retriever.com. Featuring a wealth of information and sources related to owning, training, and trialing retrievers.

www.essft.com. Devoted to all matters that involve working, field-bred English springer spaniels.